Harmony in the Home: Questions and Answers

JUSTIN BROPHY,
KATHLEEN MAGUIRE
AND
TONY BYRNE

BLACKHALL
Publishing

This book was typeset by Folio Publishing Services for

Blackhall Publishing
33 Carysfort Avenue
Blackrock
Co. Dublin
Ireland

e-mail: info@blackhallpublishing.com
www.blackhallpublishing.com

ISBN: 1 842180 99 1

A catalogue record for this book is available
from the British Library.

Printed in Ireland by
ColourBooks Ltd

CONTENTS

ACKNOWLEDGEMENTS

We give a special thanks to those men, women and young adults who shared their experiences of home life with us during our courses and seminars on *Harmony in the Home,* and during our consultations. Their honesty and courage in expressing their problems has been an immense source of inspiration to us. We thank also all those who, in one way or another, have helped us to write this book. Lelia and Gerry O'Flaherty, Emma Dunne, Anne Dunne, Esther O'Toole, Ruth Garvey, Eileen O'Brien and many other voluntary collaborators and colleagues were most generous with their time and expertise.

Dedicated
to our three families, relatives
and friends in recognition of their unstinting
love, concern and support.

Note on Answers to Legal Questions

Recourse to the law courts should be used only when everything else has failed to bring harmony, peace and security to those living in homes that are dysfunctional, disruptive or violent.

Anne Dunne, SC, one of Ireland's leading family-law barristers, has made comments on legal questions presented to her by participants at our programmes on *Harmony in the Home*. While commenting on the questions, she emphasised the importance of obtaining legal advice for each individual case, especially where property issues are concerned, and also in matters of separation and divorce, as these have such long-term consequences. Most people take considerable time and spend a lot of money preparing for marriage; the termination of a marriage warrants considerable time too.

The legal questions in this book were presented to Anne Dunne during the *Harmony in the Home* programmes and her comments on these questions are outlined here. It should be noted, however, that because little detail is given in the questions, it is difficult for her to give substantive replies in each case.

INTRODUCTION

Today many people live in circumstances that do not conform to the traditional model of home life. More common now are the two-wage-earner home, the lone-parent family, the remarriage home or the empty-nest couple whose children have grown up and moved out. Apart from these variations, large numbers of people spend part of their lives living in homes away from their families or as single young adults, divorced singles or older people who have lost their spouses. Furthermore, social and sexual rules or ethical principles that once seemed carved in stone have been set aside. However, it has to be said that a nostalgic attitude alone to this situation is inadequate and flawed.

In contemporary societies, where traditional and non-traditional models of home life prevail, there is an increasing number of problems related to divorce, lone parents and a lower rate of marriages and births. Some of these problems are reflected in the questions we are asked by participants at our courses and seminars on *Harmony in the Home,* and at our places of work. We have collated some of these questions and have suggested some possible solutions. The questions that are often presented to us include: How can I bring harmony to my home where people are in conflict? I am a lone parent with a disruptive child – what can I do? How can I help my son at home who is addicted to alcohol? How can I deal with relationship problems in my apartment? How can I help my suicidal son? Can you advise me what to do in my home to help my bad-tempered young daughter? What are my legal rights as a live-in partner? How should I address the problem of a violent husband?

We have also included techniques for dealing with serious conflict. Readers may find these useful, in part or in total, for many problems involving conflict.

We do not present this book as a panacea for problems in homes. We simply make suggestions to the readers that might help them in their search for solutions to their problems. In this respect, we recognise the wisdom of the Chinese proverb – "It is better to light a candle than curse the darkness."

Note

Every home is unique in terms of how people who live there relate or do not relate to each other and the level of psychological pain that is inflicted by disharmony or conflict. To deal with individual problems of dysfunctional homes, it is often necessary to consult a professional in the field.

We hope that this book will help to provide answers to some of the questions related to home life. However, we would like to explain that the publisher, authors and their colleagues quoted in this book disclaim liability for any pain, injury, unpleasantness, stress or any other negative reactions or outcomes that may result from the use, proper or improper, of the information, suggestions or directions in this book. We do not guarantee that the information given in the book is complete, nor should it be considered a substitute for the reader's common sense or good judgement regarding ways of addressing problems in the home.

The information in the book must not be construed or interpreted to infringe on the rights of others or to violate the laws of the land.

Harmony in the Home: Questions and Answers

Question **My husband is very controlling. I feel trapped by his controlling mentality. I am trying to keep a good relationship with him but the harmony in our home is being destroyed by his mentality. I am trying to understand why he doesn't trust me as a responsible adult. He does not like me having a night out with my female friends. He cringes when I say I would like to be involved in a local charity project. He is most inquisitive about my phone calls, text messages and mail. Please help me to deal with this problem.**

Answer No doubt you must be suffering tremendously from deep psychological pain because of your situation at home. You probably feel trapped and controlled by your husband. His controlling tactics must be gradually breaking you down. But you should not feel that it is your fault. Remember that the fault is with your husband and not with you.

You should convince yourself beyond doubt that you have a right to be free to have time out with your female friends and to be involved in a local charity if you wish to do so. Be assured that no one has a right to be inquisitive about your phone calls, text messages or mail. When you married your husband you did not surrender your basic human rights of freedom of association and movement. You are denied these rights by your husband, who is using bullying tactics. You may think that this situation will resolve itself but it will not do so unless you do something about it. You must confront your husband and regain your dignity, which is being taken away from you.

It is vital that you name what is going on between your husband and yourself. It is bullying – it has to be named as such and it has to be addressed.

You must confront your husband and tell him you are not going to take this any longer. But before you do this, you must prepare yourself for that step. You are probably at a low ebb, feeling shattered by the gradual breaking down of your self-confidence because of your husband's bullying tactics. It may be difficult for you to help yourself to feel a little stronger in yourself. However, you should try by starting to enjoy yourself and doing those things that make you feel good. Insist on doing this, whether your husband likes it or not. Talk to a trusted friend or friends and ask very frankly whether they think you are exaggerating or becoming paranoid. Cry in front of your trusted friends if you feel like it, but do not cry in front of your husband in case it confirms his sense of superiority or his perception of you as weak. You should write a diary with dates, times and places where acts of bullying by your husband have taken place. Write how you felt when you were bullied and what he said, and describe his body language. Do not exaggerate. Think about getting some professional counselling and think about going to a course on assertiveness.

Perhaps it would be a good idea to do a role-playing exercise with a trusted friend before the session to try to anticipate what your husband is likely to say or do during and after the session.

You may need to watch your body language. You may be in the habit of keeping your head down when your husband starts to bully you. Slowly change your manner, bit by bit. Look at him just above his eyes, keep your shoulders squared, walk with determined steps and do not fidget when he talks to you. If he is inclined to fold his arms when he lays down the law to you, you fold your arms too, to show him that you are not afraid of him. When he tries to limit your freedom, tell him in a slow but determined voice that you will not be denied your rights by him or anyone else. Do not shout but speak in a strong tone of voice.

When you feel good and when he looks relaxed, ask him would he fix a time when you could discuss something important with him. Decide where you would like to have this get-together. During this session, you should make sure that you control the discussion. If he tries to take over the session, remind him that you asked for the session and you need to say what you want to say. Give him the benefit of the doubt and tell him that he may not have been fully aware of how you have felt about being controlled by him, especially his becoming so inquisitive about your phone calls, mail and text messages. Tell him that you do not appreciate his negative reaction to your going out with your female friends or getting involved with a local charitable project. Tell him frankly that you need your freedom of movement and association, which is a basic human right. Explain that you will not accept any effort on his part to dominate you. You need to be trusted as a responsible adult.

He may not like what you say but you must have the courage to say it. If he shouts at you, you should keep calm. Make it clear to him that you are not prepared to be bullied.

If you come to a settlement, try to get him to agree to have a follow-up session to discuss how things have worked out. This may be difficult, but it is well worth trying.

However, if your husband is not willing to discuss the problem or if he will not change his bullying tactics, and if the situation becomes more difficult for you, then you will have to consider other options. One of those options may be mediation (see pages 118–119).

Question   My husband and I want to have a happy home but we feel we are failing somehow. We believe that it is important to keep a clean, neat and tidy home where we could invite visitors without embarrassment. Our teenage children don't seem to see the importance of having a home with those kinds of standards. They seldom put things in their proper places, leave dirty mugs all over the sitting room, never wipe their feet when they enter the house and leave cushions and magazines on the floor. Their bedrooms are very untidy, dirty and look a bit like a health hazard. All this is causing tension and friction. Have you any suggestions to address the problem?

Answer   Obviously this is a worrying problem for you and your husband. It must cause you a lot of upset and distress. Perhaps it might help if you and your husband would think about certain important points. There is a difference between a house and a home. A house is a building with a foundation, walls and a roof. In such a building there is no difficulty in having everything in its proper place and looking spic and span. The carpets are kept clean, there are no unwashed mugs all over the sitting room and the cushions are placed neatly on the settee. Everything can be kept in perfect condition with the smell of polish purifying the air in the house. But a home is a very different place. It responds to that ache in the human heart for a space where people can be as they are and not be questioned. It is that sacred space where people, with all their imperfections, can experience love, comfort, security and peace. It is where people constantly interact and where relationships are formed, maintained and developed. But living in a confined space can cause tension, friction and sometimes even stress. Nevertheless, in the home, relationships are developed and maintained despite the occasional misunderstandings and squabbles.

You and your husband have equal rights with your teenage children regarding having peace and comfort in your home. So your teenagers must honour their obligation to see that your rights are respected. It has to be realised that if harmony and peace are to prevail there must be a compromise. Perhaps a possible solution would come about through dialogue: maybe it could be agreed that areas in the home used by all the family should be kept neat and tidy. These areas would be the kitchen, dining room, bathroom and sitting room. It would be advisable to encourage teenagers and young adults to keep their own areas in the home basically clean.

Question   **My wife has a serious drinking problem. What can I do to motivate her to get professional help? She is reluctant to seek help.**

Answer   It would be advisable for you to show your wife as much compassion, love and understanding as possible. She needs it badly because of her addiction to alcohol. When she is sober try to have an open discussion with her about her problem. Use "I" statements. For example, make statements such as, "I wonder could you help me because I am so worried that you might become sick if you continue to drink a lot." This kind of approach will show better results than saying, "You are becoming a drunkard. You must stop drinking too much."

I am sure you will realise that it will not help your wife if you denounce her, make her feel guilty, moralise about her problem, call her an alcoholic or become aggressive with her. Remember, her conduct when she is sober is probably different to her conduct when she is under the influence of drink.

Keep giving her reasons for hoping that one day she will solve the problem with a little professional assistance and your loving support. Tell her she is not alone and that together you will work things out. There will be two stages that she has to go through: one is the discovery stage and the other is the recovery stage. In the discovery stage she has to become acutely aware of the negative effects of misusing alcohol. Some of these negative effects are a general decline in physical and mental health, loss of the powers of reasoning, memory decline, loss of control of language, mood swings, depression, obesity, liver and stomach problems, risks of unconsciousness, total dependency on alcohol, withdrawal symptoms, risk to nervous system, damage to brain cells, high blood pressure and skin problems. Besides these negative effects, there are the financial difficulties caused by the alcohol addiction, risks to home and married life, loss of relatives or friends and possible difficulties with the law because of drink-driving or fighting under the influence of drink.

It takes some time for most people who misuse alcohol to realise what is happening to them as they keep increasing their intake of drink. They do not fully realise how alcohol misuse gradually starts to destroy their lives. For many it is a process of discovery based on their experience of intoxication.

Hopefully when your wife goes through the discovery stage, she will progress to the recovery stage. You should be on the lookout for events that might encourage her to arrive at this stage. Events that might trigger this process could be a health scare, a serious drink-related accident or difficulties with the law. When she arrives at this stage you should encourage her to go with you to the family doctor. Perhaps you should have a confidential chat with the doctor to discuss your wife's problem and the urgency of this important moment when she has agreed to seek professional help. The doctor may arrange for her to get some professional counselling with an addiction counsellor, or therapy in a clinic, or to have her admitted to a hospital.

It is important that you, as your wife's carer, should take care of yourself. Do not blame yourself for this problem. Do not think that you can cure your wife. You can help her but she is the only one who can solve her problem. You may also be inadvertently prolonging and adding to the problem and you need to realise how this may involve changing yourself and how you have handled the situation up to now. Be conscious of your limitations. Do not be too upset if there is a setback during the recovery stage. Your wife may return to some of her old habits but regard that as a "slip", not a "fall". Perhaps it would be good to contact Al-Anon, AA or the local alcohol counselling service to ask them for advice and documentation on how you can help your wife.

Finally, it is important not to allow the problem to encourage *you* to drink to excess. It can happen that people who try to help those close to them to overcome alcohol misuse can become addicted themselves.

Question   One of our neighbours is becoming very intrusive. She seems to expect us to open our home to her when she knocks at our door. My partner and I are private people. We don't want to be rude to this lady and have a bad relationship with her but we don't want her to feel that she can come in for a chat and a cup of tea at any time. We realise she is lonely and we feel obliged to be kind to her. Have you any suggestions as to what we should do?

Answer   There are different models of homes. Some of them have an open-door policy for visitors. People in these homes consider it an honour and a blessing to have visitors. They love to entertain, have a chat and share food and drink with guests. There is a warm welcome for uninvited visitors, especially neighbours. This type of home has little or no strict time-frame for meals or other home events. Visitors are given precedence over television programmes, especially soap operas. This model is not uncommon in rural areas. However, even there it is becoming less common.

Another model of home is the "private castle" home where privacy is a priority. Unannounced visitors are looked on as intruders. Meal times are adhered to strictly. People in these homes want to be alone and regard their homes as sacred sanctuaries, reserved for family members only or for those who are formally invited. In these homes, favourite television programmes must never be put aside for drop-in visitors. Neighbours who make uninvited visits to this model of home can be intrusive and cause a breakdown of relationships.

It is important for you to explain politely and sensitively to your neighbour that you and your partner feel the need to be alone together but it would be good to let her know that she should feel free to phone you if she needs something urgently. Let her know that you are there for her when there is an emergency.

While identifying and respecting the two models of homes, it has to be said that it appears strange if a home is totally exclusive and secluded, and never has visitors. A home should ideally be a sacred space where people share with other people, not only with family members but also with people from the wider community.

Question   **Our new neighbours park their car
outside our home. For the past
twenty-two years we have used that
space to park our car. Can we do anything legally to solve this problem?**

Answer   The use of a car space outside a resi-
dence is often the cause of a breakdown
of relationships between neighbours.
You have used the space outside your
home for the past twenty-two years and
naturally you feel you should be allowed
to continue to do so. Unfortunately, you
have no legal right to the space. The
road is public and unless there are local
authority restrictions there is not a lot that
can be done. However, you might try to
make a humble request to the new
neighbours to allow you to park the car
there out of the goodness of their hearts,
emphasising that you are aware that you
do not have a legal right in the matter. If
this is unsuccessful, you should talk to
the local authority.

Question   **Our new neighbours are non-nationals.
                  Since their arrival there is a certain
                  amount of anxiety in our home
                  because we do not know how to
                  approach them. Can you advise us?**

Answer   It is normal for people to experience
                  uncertain emotions when they encounter
                  strangers. These emotions can be inten-
                  sified by a lack of familiarity with your
                  neighbours' culture, which can lead to an
                  inability to communicate with them. This
                  makes relationships very difficult. Hence
                  it is understandable that you are experi-
                  encing some anxiety in your home.

                  A practical way of overcoming the
                  anxiety would be to engage in an exciting
                  and informative process of discovery by
                  learning more about the language, his-
                  tory, culture and music of your neigh-
                  bours' home country. It would be most
                  helpful if you offered your neighbours the
                  opportunity to explore the Irish language,
                  history, culture and music.

                  This process of exploration and famil-
                  iarity may be slow. Perhaps it could
                  begin with a welcoming card and flowers
                  to your new neighbours. It might help the
                  process if you invited your neighbours'
                  children to your children's birthday par-
                  ties. This would be a great ice-breaker.

                  It would be useful to remember an old
                  Irish saying: "With us there are no
                  strangers, only friends we have not met."

Question   **My husband is addicted to cannabis and when he is under the influence of the drug he is a danger to our two young children and to me. He acts in a crazy manner and frightens the children and me. I need to have him barred from the home. What steps should I take?**

Answer   This is a very painful situation for you to be in, and to see your children so frightened must be very distressing. To reach the conclusion that your only option is to have your husband barred is understandable. Hopefully it will be comforting to know that you are entitled to the protection of the law. The Domestic Violence Act, 1996, provides remedies to adults and children in situations where violence, whether physical or psychological, is involved. No person has the right or entitlement to harm another and this is particularly so in the case of children. Parents and adults generally must protect children, and parents in particular must ensure that harm is not caused to them.

In some circumstances one person may be prepared to endure harm or injury from another. However, legally, they have no right to allow a situation to prevail where children are harmed or frightened. To allow any person under the influence of a drug to cause fear or hurt to adults or children is unacceptable on the part of a wife and mother, who is under an obligation to ensure that proper protective steps are taken to prevent such behaviour.

Under the Domestic Violence Act, a Court application may be made to prevent such violent and "crazy" behaviour. If necessary, an Order could be obtained to exclude or bar the offender from the home in which the family resides. The application should be made to the District Court, which is the Court empowered with criminal sanctions, but such applications may also be made to the Circuit or High Courts. Staff members in the District Court office will provide help to people making applications to the Court. It is not necessary to have legal representation but in serious applications, such as a barring application where the evidence is contested, it is advisable to do so. Under the Domestic Violence Act any one of four remedies may be granted by the Court, as follows:

Safety Order
Parents and guardians of children must protect them by making an application to Court, if necessary. A Safety Order restrains the offending person from using or threatening to use violence, from molesting or putting in fear the person seeking relief on their own behalf or on behalf of a child or children. It restrains the person, if they are not residing at the place where the applicant is residing, from watching or besetting that place. A specific application for a Safety Order

must be made to the Court and, where no such application is made, the Court is not entitled to make the Order.

Where an applicant is afraid to make an application to the Court on behalf of a child or children, the Health Service Executive has power to do so where such authority is satisfied that a risk exists. Where a child is eighteen years of age or over but suffers a disability, as a consequence of which dependency continues, the Court will grant an Order for the safety of that person as well as other children. The Order will remain in place for the dependent person as long as the dependency lasts, but not for longer than five years, when another application for a further order may be sought.

Protection Order
A Protection Order may be obtained where an application for a Barring Order has been made to the Court but has not yet been granted. The Protection Order remains in place until the barring application is determined by the Court, when it automatically lapses. A Protection Order may be granted by the Court in the absence of the respondent.

Barring Order
An application for a Barring Order must be specifically sought from the Court and will be granted where the Court is satisfied that sufficient evidence exists to bar

the respondent from the home where the applicant and dependent children ordinarily reside. The Court will hear the evidence of each party, applicant and respondent, as well as any relevant witnesses. Where the Order is made, the respondent is required to leave the premises and they cannot return without leave of the Court. The applicant is not entitled to permit a return, as any such permission, if acted upon, will result in a lapse of the Order.

Once notice of the Order is served on the respondent, it immediately becomes operative and any breach is a criminal offence. The Gardaí may arrest the person breaching the Order and prosecute the matter before a criminal court. Once a Court Order is made, a copy will be provided to the person seeking the Order, a copy will be served on the person against whom the Order has been obtained and the Gardaí will be provided with a copy of the Order. If the Health Service Executive, formerly known as the Health Board, or other Authority is involved in the application, a copy will be provided to the relevant Authority. Where a respondent on whom a copy of a barring application has been served fails or refuses to attend Court for the hearing, the Court will still hear the application provided that it is satisfied that the person concerned has been validly served with the application.

Interim Barring Order

In very exceptional circumstances, an
Interim Barring Order may be granted by
the Court where it is of the view that very
significant danger exists to the applicant
or dependent children pending the hearing of the Barring Order application.
Such an Interim Order will be granted for
only a number of days so that the Court
will be given evidence as soon as possible for a full Barring Order.

A breach of a District Court Order is a
criminal offence but breaches of Safety,
Protection, Interim Barring or Barring
Orders made by the Circuit or High
Courts are civil matters and require an
application to be made to the relevant
Court to find the person in breach of the
Order to be in contempt of the Court.

An application may be made to the
Court making the Order to vary or discharge the Order. In District Court cases,
notification must be given to the Gardaí
of any variation or discharge granted.

An Interim Barring or Barring Order
prevents the person against whom it is
made from threatening the applicant at
work or by telephone. Where a person
against whom an Order is made was
present in Court when the Order was
made, the person is bound by the order
and no further notification is necessary.
In circumstances where the person was
not present, notification by the applicant
is sufficient. However, difficulties could
arise if a breach occurred where a copy

of the Order has not been served and a claim is made that no notification had been served.

The Courts are careful to protect family members and dependent children in particular and the Domestic Violence Act has been enacted for that purpose. It should be used in all situations of damage and harm and, in particular, in such a case as outlined in the question.

Question   There are four of us renting an apart-
                  ment where there is little peace or har-
                  mony. The apartment is reasonably
                  priced and convenient to my work.
                  I don't want to leave it. The main prob-
                  lem is that some flatmates use sup-
                  plies of food or drink that belong to
                  the other people in the apartment and
                  don't replace these supplies. Very
                  often lights or the cooker are left on
                  when not in use. The noise from tele-
                  visions, radios and CD players makes
                  sleep impossible at night. Have you
                  any suggestions that could solve
                  these problems?

Answer   The situation in your home does not help
                  you to find peace and harmony there. It
                  would seem that the four of you living in
                  this home need to have more dialogue to
                  reach an agreement on matters related
                  to food, drinks, use of electricity and the
                  noise levels from televisions, radios and
                  CD players.
                      Most adults who live together in
                  homes are reasonable people but they
                  may not act in a reasonable way if there
                  are no regulations in place and no real
                  dialogue on what is expected of each
                  one in the home. Clearly defined bound-
                  aries must be identified and agreed on
                  by each person.
                      Possibly each of you finds the present
                  situation unpleasant but no one may
                  want to initiate discussions – resulting in
                  everyone trying to be polite about the sit-

uation. For that reason, you might suggest to the others in the apartment to have a short, informal get-together to discuss some basic matters related to the home.

You should also arrange a date for a follow-up meeting, to see if some fine-tuning of the decisions made at the first meeting is needed. If the situation in your home does not improve you may need to look for alternative accommodation. This may be inconvenient for you but it could be the best option – life is too short to be unhappy and not at peace.

Question   **Our home is being disturbed by our
neighbours, who play loud music into
the early hours of the morning, disturbing the peace in our home. Despite a
request by the Gardaí to turn down the
music, these neighbours continue to
disturb us with the loud music. Can the
law help us to solve the problem?**

Answer   It is important for the sake of peace and
harmony to have good relationships with
your neighbours. When there are bad
feelings, the problems can intensify and
result in an increase of upset and distress. Hence, every effort to solve the
problem of loud music should be made
before seeking help from the law, for fear
that it might make the situation worse.

The playing of loud music at unsocia-
ble hours on a regular basis could consti-
tute a nuisance and a court application to
restrain this nuisance is possible. If the
Gardaí have intervened and the noise
continues, it might be wise for you to
consider making an application to the
District Court. An order would be made
by the Court if it was satisfied that a nuisance was being caused. If there is a
breach of such an order, the Court can
hold the noisemakers responsible and
make orders accordingly. Continued
breaches could result in imprisonment.

Friction between neighbours is
extremely difficult to control. However, it is
vital for you to keep within the law yourself
and avoid vengeful counter-attacking
options that would worsen the situation.

Question   New neighbours have moved into the house next to ours. They have set up a car-repair business and have customers' cars in their garden and outside their home and ours. This is causing a lot of tension between the two families. Do we have any legal rights to help us solve the problem?

Answer   It seems that the neighbours in this case are in breach of the planning laws, in that they are conducting a business from a residential location. Unfortunately, parking cars on their property or on the public thoroughfare is not something that can be controlled because people cannot really interfere with what other people do in their gardens, unless it is noisy or otherwise causing a nuisance. If there is interference by way of noise or trespass onto your property by water or other items, then an application to the District Court on the grounds of nuisance would be appropriate. Notification, verbally as well as in writing, should be given, with a request that the behaviour cease. However, as we all know, rows with neighbours are notoriously difficult to deal with.

It is advisable that you avoid any action or verbal exchange with your neighbours that could complicate the situation and lead you into legal difficulties.

Question   I married four years ago and brought my wife into my home, which I owned. Unfortunately, we began to experience serious problems in our relationship and, three months after our marriage, she left me and went to live with another man, where she still is. Now I have a new partner. What rights does my wife have over the ownership of my house?

Answer   This is a problem that may cause a lot of upset and distress to three people: yourself, your wife and your new partner. So it is important to address the problem with great compassion and sensitivity.

As regards the law, if the house is owned outright without a mortgage, the partner cannot acquire a beneficial interest in the house.

If the house is fully paid for by the husband and there was no mortgage when he married, his wife will not acquire a beneficial interest in the home. Furthermore, three months is a very short period – if your ex-wife had lived with you for longer she may have had more of a claim to the property. As a spouse, the wife's consent will be required in the sale of the family home. However, it is difficult to advise where information is limited and I would recommend that legal advice should be obtained.

Question   I own a house where I have been living with my partner for four years.
She gave birth to our son two years
ago. Serious problems have arisen
between my partner and I. We want to
separate. I wonder what legal rights
and obligations I have with regard to
my son's maintenance. How often can
I see him? Do I have to support my
partner? Please advise me.

Answer   There is no legal obligation on a man to
support a woman to whom he is not mar-
ried. The only obligation is to maintain
the child as long as that child remains
dependent or until he reaches sixteen
years of age, if no longer in education.
The question of access to be exercised
is a matter to be worked out between the
parties, or by Court Order if necessary.
Access usually takes place at least once
a week, or more frequently.

Question   **My wife and I have agreed, after many years of tension, conflict and arguing, that it is not good for us to live together any more as husband and wife. We feel it is better for the two of us to separate and, more especially, it is better for our two children. We want to do it with the least expense because we have limited resources. What would you advise us to do?**

Answer   The decision made by you and your wife to separate is no doubt adding to the emotional pain you have experienced over many years of conflict and tension.

With regard to your concern about the expense involved in the process of separation, it may help you to know that free mediation services are provided by the State to enable families to resolve difficulties and such services also provide assistance in separation and divorce situations. Assistance will be provided by qualified counsellors to work out terms acceptable to both parties and such terms as may be ruled on by Court or encompassed in an agreement executed by the two parties. Since separation and divorce are very grave steps affecting the future lives of adults and children, it is wise to seek legal advice but it is not obligatory to do so. Court applications may be made by parties without legal involvement and, where resources are restricted, careful consideration should be given to embarking on such far-reaching steps.

Separation is always painful, no matter what the circumstances. You, your wife and especially the children may need aftercare to help you to cope. These services are available from many voluntary agencies (see Appendix).

Question   **My wife and I have been living together for forty-five years. Recently, my wife has often been bringing up the topic of our advancing age and our future. I turn off when she does this and she becomes mad with me. There is tension in our home because of this. Have you any suggestions as to how we should address our problem?**

Answer   It is understandable that you fear getting older, but there is no need to be afraid of the future if you make good plans to ensure you will enjoy happiness in your later years. The future is very uncertain but it is most important to make provisions while you are well and your mental faculties are sound. To avoid difficulties in your golden years, it is advisable for you to consult a solicitor to ensure that your will is in order, your savings are secure and that someone is given the power of attorney in the event of your not being mentally or physically capable of handling your financial affairs, home and property.

You would be advised to have another clause stipulating that your will must not be altered without the knowledge and physical presence of specified trusted people with the power of attorney. This will protect you from being coerced into making a change in your will.

Regarding where you will reside in the years ahead, you might like to consider the following options.

Staying in Your Own Home
If you decide to live out your life in your own home, then you should now make it as user-friendly as possible. You should arrange your home and garden so there will be a minimum amount of maintenance. Switches, lights, plugs and appliances should be in places for easy accessibility and use. Make sure you have a reliable alarm system, panic button and a hands-free and mobile phone.

Special Housing
The second option for you to consider is to live in a special housing facility for elderly people that has secure living, catering, laundry and nursing care. If you decide to take this option, you should do so while you are still active.

Nursing Home
The third option is to reside in a nursing home. Visit a number of these homes to find out the prices and conditions in each. Find out what it is really like to live in these homes as a resident.

Special Arrangement
The fourth option is to consult your bank manager and find out what the bank or other institutions offer by way of selling your home on the condition that you and your wife have a legal right to live there for the rest of your lives. The money you receive from this special sale of your home should be wisely invested for your

upkeep in your old age. It would be good to be clear on who is legally responsible for the maintenance of the house while you are living there.

Family Moving in With You
Another option would be that some of your family members could move in with you. This may not be easy and if you take this option, you must have legal protection that you will not be expected to be an unpaid baby-sitter or childminder, that you and your wife will have your privacy and that your independence will be secure. You also need a stipulation that your friends will have access to your home.

When you and your wife have made decisions to secure your future, you will find that you will be able to live together more peacefully and harmony will be restored in your home.

Question   **My wife and I have completely different interests in sports, politics and
religious matters. We have a good
relationship in general but it is being
overshadowed by these different
interests. Please help us to address
these problems.**

Answer   Different interests in sports, politics and
religion between you and your wife could
cause feelings of estrangement, remote-
ness or even alienation. When people
have no interest in a topic and it is discussed by others for long periods of time,
it can cause tension and boredom.
However, with serious reflection and
good understanding these feelings need
not cause a difficulty with the relationship
you and your wife have in your home.

Perhaps you should give some
thought to the following points. No two
people are exactly the same. If they
were, life would be very boring. The old
saying is still valid: variety is the spice of
life. Furthermore, you should remember
that you and your wife did not marry
each other because of your common
interests in sports, politics and religion;
you married because you loved each
other.

That love can develop by accepting
and respecting each other's differences.
It would be advisable for you and your
wife to identify matters of common interest and to focus on these areas and
enjoy them together.

Question   **My husband and I are having serious
problems with our sex life. He can be
very demanding. He becomes angry
when I tell him that I am too tired or
not feeling well when he wants to
have sex with me. How could I help
him to be more reasonable? This
problem causes a lot of disharmony
and tension in our home.**

Answer   The situation you describe is very common. It sounds as if sex has become an
afterthought in your marriage rather than
an essential part of the fun and intimacy
of the relationship. Perhaps your husband has become too busy or too tired to
set aside any time for you. He may see
sex as a shortcut to the intimacy that you
formerly enjoyed and as a reasonable
and essential part of married life. Is it
possible that you have become overly
preoccupied with family responsibilities
and have neglected your own needs and
the time you need to spend together?

It is easy for this to happen as children's demands, caring for elderly relatives and the normal pressures of work
and social life intensify in the middle
years of a marriage. Your sex life can
either survive or wither during this
period. The only way it will survive is if
you both agree that it is something you
want to nurture. You should then agree
how to do this. It may seem a little con-
trived to sit down and discuss it, but it
could help to solve the problem. The old

reliables of a quiet setting, a lovely din-
ner, a good bottle of wine and a bit of privacy are sometimes left out as the
marriage goes on. If the two of you find
time to set aside for these kinds of
opportunities, and also for the possibility
of spontaneity, the intimacy and joy that
sexuality brought to your marriage will
return.

Question My husband is a highly qualified professional who is totally dedicated to his profession. I am not so well qualified and know little or nothing about his profession. He often talks about his work and uses terms that I don't understand. When he invites his colleagues to a party in our home, the discussion is usually about professional matters. I feel totally alienated and lost. This embarrasses me and it is causing tension in our home. What can be done to solve this problem?

Answer The fact that you do not have the same profession as your husband could be a great help to both of you. Everyone needs variety in their lives. We all need to transcend the parameters of our own mind-sets and views. Your husband needs you to help him get in touch with the realities outside of his profession. It is not psychologically healthy for him to be totally absorbed in professional matters.

You and your husband should become aware that you did not marry each other for his profession – you married because you loved each other. That love has to be nurtured as the years pass on.

It might be helpful for you if you and your husband identified some areas of common interest, e.g. outdoor activities, that would be healthy for both of you.

Your husband may not fully realise that not everyone knows the meaning of those professional terms he uses.

Perhaps you might ask him to explain these terms in simple language. Writing out a list of these terms and their meanings could help you to understand him better.

You and your husband should reach some kind of agreement about the parties in your home. Maybe he could agree not to talk about professional matters until after the meal. Afterwards he and his friends could talk as long as they like about business.

You might find it helpful to invite your friends who are not from your husband's profession to the parties. After the meal you and your friends could get together and have your own relaxing and enjoyable conversation.

Question   **My wife does not communicate very well. There are long periods of silence. When I ask her what she thinks about any issue, she replies, "I don't know." She tends to stare into space, looks lost at times, rarely smiles, hates going out for a meal and can be very abrupt. When we first married she wasn't like that. What can I do?**

Answer   Silence and detachment are very difficult to deal with. It sounds as if things have changed for the worse for her. It is quite possible that she has become disillusioned, withdrawn and shut off from ordinary family encounters. This is sometimes symptomatic of depression. A person with depression may also have difficulty sleeping at night, maintaining interest in everyday things and coping with ordinary expectations.

However, there may be another reason why she is behaving like this and it is important to find out why this is. It may take considerable patience. You both must set aside time in which you can communicate with each other in a relaxed and undisturbed manner. Sometimes going for a walk is a good way to get a person to talk. Direct grilling will not work, however. You must be very persistent but not in a bullying way. You should express concern for her well-being, remind her of her previous happiness and express optimism that things can change for the better. It is possible that she does not want to burden anyone with what is troubling her or she may feel that it would be too upsetting for other people to hear. Indicating that you are strong and ready to hear what she may need to say would be a great help to her. A trusted friend or family member may also be able to help.

If this fails, coaxing her to visit her GP would be important.

Question   In general, my wife and I get on well
together, but we have some problems
that need to be addressed. My wife
tends to spend too much on clothes
and groceries. She constantly sug-
gests that we should have one or two
holidays each year. She does not
seem to realise that we cannot afford
all the expenses. She becomes very
tearful and upset when I try to explain
that we do not have enough money to
meet her shopping sprees and her
desire to have holidays abroad. All
this is causing tension between us
and a lot of pain. How can I handle
this problem?

Answer   It would appear that you and your wife
have a good relationship, despite the
present situation. If that were not so, she
would not want to go on holidays with
you. You say she overspends on groceries but those groceries are not for her
alone. Maybe she is spending money
like this to make you happy, preparing
food you enjoy. She overspends on
clothes, but could you give her the benefit of the doubt and presume that she is
doing this to make herself more attractive to you and help you to be proud of
how well she looks?

The problem in your home may be
more   about   communication   than
finances. Perhaps, for one reason or
another, your wife has not been sufficiently informed about the actual income

in the home. When both of you are feeling relaxed and in good form, you should ask her to arrange a time when you can help plan the finances of the home with her. During this get-together, you should discuss the financial plan for the next year in terms of income and expenditure.

Hopefully your wife will realise what money will be available for holidays when all the essential items of expenditure have been identified. It might be good to keep in mind that weekly budget reviews are especially helpful – if somewhat tedious. Saving is the main route out of the enslavement of debt and poverty.

Question   I am receiving text messages from an
               unknown source stating that my part-
               ner of seven years is having an affair
               with a married man who is her boss at
               the office. I don't want to believe that
               this is true but I am suspicious of her
               because she arrives home very late at
               night and says that she has to work
               overtime in the office. She seems to
               be losing interest in me and in our six-
               year-old child. Tension is growing
               between us. I don't want to challenge
               her in case I make the situation worse.
               What do you think I should do?

Answer   You have to address the situation in your
               home. You have no choice – you owe it
               to yourself and, more especially, to your
               child to find out what is going on.

               Perhaps you could ask your partner to
               have a quiet chat with you when she is
               not too tired and when both of you feel
               relaxed. During that time, talk to her
               about the good times you had together in
               the past. Reassure her that you want her
               to be happy in the home and that you
               also want to be happy. Speak about your
               child and how you both love this child.
               Acknowledge that she works very hard
               and because of her overtime she comes
               home very late. Tell her that you are wor-
               ried because you feel she is losing inter-
               est in you and your child. Explain that it
               is causing you a lot of tension and worry.
               Say that this tension has become more
               serious because of the text messages

you are receiving. Tell her that you do not want to believe these messages that say she is having an affair with her boss because the person who is sending the messages does not identify themselves. Ask her if she has any idea who is sending the messages. Her response will help you to clear the air and hopefully it will help you to know how to deal with the situation. A guilty conscience loves to confess, so be ready for anything that you might hear.

Question   **We have only one bank account for our home and it is controlled solely by my partner. I have asked him to make arrangements with the bank so that I can withdraw money to meet essential household and personal expenses. He has refused to do so. He does not give me a fixed amount for household expenses and for other expenses to do with our two children and me. All this is creating a lot of tension in our home. I feel he does not trust me; I feel like a beggar every time I have to ask for money. These bad feelings are destroying the harmony in our home. What should I do about it?**

Answer   It cannot be easy for you in a situation like this. You feel mistrusted and your difficult task of looking after the two children and the home is not fully appreciated by your partner, who makes you feel like you are begging when you ask for the money you need to run the home.

Perhaps it would be advisable for you to speak with your husband at an appropriate time about your deep pain at not being trusted by him. It sometimes happens that people are not aware of the pain they inflict on others by not trusting them.

From our experience of helping people in your situation, we have realised that many partners have no idea what it costs to buy food and clothing, pay medical, heating and cooking bills, school fees and books, pocket money and so on. They do not seem to realise how degrading it can be for someone to have to ask for essential money every time they need to pay for running a home and caring for the children and themselves. We have found that some people think that everything can be paid from the children's allowance.

You should keep receipts for every item of expenditure. Work out the costs for two weeks. Add 10 per cent for unforeseen expenses. Ask for a get-together with your partner to discuss financial matters. Show him the receipts and the account of expenditures. Tell him very politely but firmly that he has to decide with you how he is going to meet the expenses. Ask him to consider the following options.

He might like to open a joint account and give you authorisation with the bank to draw money from the account.

If he does not want to do that, he might consider getting you a debit card on his account.

If he is not happy to do that, he should agree that you can open your own account and he will set up a standing order with his bank to pay the required amount every month into your account.

He has to decide which option he would like to take but you must tell him that you have decided that you will not continue to accept the current financial situation. Perhaps you should give him a few days to make his decision but tell him that you need him to take action within a week, whatever option he decides to take.

Question   **My husband works many hours of
overtime in his office and has a very
good income. He leaves the house at
7 a.m. and comes home at midnight at
least three times a week. I'm left at
home to look after our three young
children. I feel lonely and at times
rejected. What should I do?**

Answer   The situation in your home is very difficult and stressful. It might be helpful for
you and your husband to have a few
hours together in a quiet and relaxed situation to look at the problem using a simple method of reflection.

The first step in this method is to
describe how you and your husband are
feeling about the problem in your home.
The description of the problem should be
in great detail and an agreement should
be reached on it.

The second step is to list in writing all
the positive dimensions of your husband
working long hours and receiving a good
income but resulting in your feelings of
loneliness and rejection. As you identify
the positive points, you should not argue,
challenge or discuss them.

The third step is to write down all the
negative points of your husband working
for long hours. Once again, do not discuss or argue about these points.

The fourth step is to reflect in silence
on the two lists. If you are religious people, perhaps you might like to pray
together at this stage for a few moments.

After the time of reflection, you should discuss the positive and negative points, as you and your husband might need clarification of them.

The fifth step is to evaluate the points – not in terms of the number of points for the positive and negative dimensions, but in terms of the importance of each point.

The sixth step in the process is to attempt to reach a solution to the problem. To do this, both of you may have to compromise a little. It may be that each of you will have to give up a little of what you think should be the solution.

Each of you must make a commitment to implement the decision you have reached. It is advisable to arrange a follow-up session to discuss the result of the implementation of your decisions. This method has been used by many people and the results have been very satisfactory. It would be worthwhile trying it out.

Question   **Four years ago my husband was unfaithful to me. He has since repented and asked me to forgive him. I have done so but I cannot forget what happened and I am finding it difficult to relate closely to him. What do I need to do to overcome this problem?**

Answer   Your feelings are entirely understandable. The details of his infidelity are not clear, but undoubtedly the more you think about what happened, the more upset you will become. If it was a repeated betrayal of your trust, it is understandable that you are suspicious of his repentance. Realistically, it may take years for your intimacy to recover and it's important that you both understand this. If it was a less calculated indiscretion, you may not need to be so mistrustful but your feelings will be no less injured.

Many men repent after such incidents but are not always sincere, and you need to be vigilant but not preoccupied with what he is doing now. Allowing a period of detachment will clarify the matter as to whether he really is committed to an exclusive relationship with you in the future or whether he is just suiting himself.

For your own part, it is important not to enquire endlessly into or dwell on any knowledge you have of what happened. Try not to let it undermine your self-esteem, lead you to neglecting yourself or regard that part of your life as over.

You should use the opportunity to enhance your own life and self-regard until you feel confident about yourself again. When you have achieved this you will be better able to renegotiate intimacy and you will have established whether or not he is worthy of your trust again.

Your husband must use the time to deepen his own understanding of his human frailty and its destructive capacity. He must demonstrate repeatedly and unambiguously his commitment to the relationship despite the cooling-off in intimacy. He is not entitled to let his anger and frustration further disturb your relationship, as he must learn to pay a price for his betrayal.

All that said, it is important to remember that forgiveness is the point at which love is created and strengthened, and you mustn't let what has happened rob you of this joy-giving and renewing intimacy, which is a fundamental part of your marriage.

Question   **Relations between my wife and I are at a low ebb. We seem to be experiencing a lot of serious conflict lately. I feel that if we don't do something about this problem we will have to separate. We are very private people and do not wish to invite a third person to deal with the problem. Could you recommend any way of helping us to save our marriage and to make our home peaceful?**

Answer   Serious conflict that causes your relationship to be so strained is no doubt very painful for you and your wife. You are fortunate, though, that you both realise the seriousness of the problem and desire to do something to improve it before it causes further damage to your relationship. You may be able to solve your problem without having recourse to a third party. A good starting point for you might be to reflect on the following ideas about conflict and how to address it.

Conflict exists when two or more people perceive that their interests are incompatible and express hostile attitudes or take action that damages the ability of the other party to pursue their interests. Many people do not realise that conflict in homes is a common experience. The majority of homes experience conflict. This may be cold comfort for you, but at least you know that you are not alone.

Most people in homes want to communicate well but, unfortunately, many have never learned to communicate when it counts most, i.e. in conflict. The key to addressing conflict is to know how to communicate. "Conflict is the midwife of awareness and growth."[1] If it is handled badly, it can destroy relationships; however, if it is handled well, relationships can grow and deepen through it. Knowing how to handle conflict is essential to creating harmony in a home.

When we are experiencing conflict we may react, which means we lose our temper, shout, explode or blame. This sort of behaviour does not in any way solve conflict. It makes a bad situation worse. We can, instead, respond by saying something such as, "So we have a difference of opinion. Can we try to recognise each other's feelings on the matter? Let's do so calmly and with respect for each other." Responding rather than reacting is the best way to deal with conflict. You should ask yourself regularly, "When I am in conflict with my wife do I respond or do I react?" You must understand and believe that handling conflict well is critical to harmony in the home and communicating well is critical to handling conflict.

If you want to create a happy and peaceful home where relationships grow and deepen, one of the most powerful things you can do is to reflect on what often happens when people are in conflict.

Conflict in homes can arise when problems or difficulties are exaggerated

---

[1] Statement by Paolo Freire (lecture at Boston University, 1983).

beyond all proportion. A typical example of this can be seen when one person simply says, "I'm tired of cleaning and polishing this house." That simple statement can trigger a nasty response, such as, "Oh, for heaven's sake, you're always complaining. Do you think I never do anything in this home? I am fed up with you. I would be better off out of here." At a time like this, nasty comments are thrown back and forth at each other. Once very nasty or verbally abusive comments are made, they are very hard to take back. However, you must not lose heart. Very often the remarks made during these kinds of arguments do not reflect what one person actually feels about the other. Rather, the hurtful words may be weapons used in a desperate effort of self-defence. In a heated argument, we can say things that we afterwards regret. Try to keep in mind that all this happens when issues are blown out of all proportion.

How can you handle a situation like this? Well, you might like to try what is called "short-circuiting". Steer yourself positively out of the situation by softening your voice and trying to understand the other person's point of view. This is a powerful tool you can use to defuse tension. If you feel things are getting out of hand, just stop talking and take some time out. Sit quietly, have a cup of tea or go for a walk.

It often happens when people are in conflict that one person subtly or directly puts down the thoughts, feelings or character of the other. Such behaviour, whether intentional or not, is devastating and destroys the self-esteem and self-confidence of the targeted person. Another subtle form of putting down someone is ignoring something good that is done by the targeted person at a time when that person is expecting praise. Instead of praise, a minor problem is highlighted. Going out of your way to do helpful things and being ignored and criticised for your efforts is very painful. The targeted person in situations like this will probably tend to cover up who they are and what they think, because it seems too risky to do otherwise. This kind of behaviour is like a poison to the well-being of relationships and destroys harmony in the home.

The best way for you to avoid putting people down is to give the utmost respect to the character, views and feelings of other persons. The one raising the concern should be respected and heard. Of course respecting another person's views does not mean that you must agree with that person's viewpoint. Respecting other people's views is a powerful tool that you can use both to deepen relationships and reduce tension, resentment or anger. To avoid putting down someone is certainly not easy when you are angry and frustrated; however, when you work on it you will be surprised at the successful outcome.

When two people are in a conflict, it may happen that one of them will be unwilling to participate in or stay with important discussions about the problem. Withdrawal can be as subtle as just switching off during an argument or it can be more obvious, for example simply walking out of a room. The withdrawer may tend to become quiet during an argument or may quickly agree to some suggestion just to end the conversation without the slightest mention of a follow-through. In a conflict one party may avoid or be reluctant to participate in a discussion or even to prevent the conversation from happening in the first place. The person who is prone to avoidance would be happier if the difficult topic never came up for discussion and, if it did, they would show the signs of withdrawal mentioned above. There can be a process where one person pursues the problem and the other withdraws. Both parties act and react in a sort of tit-for-tat fashion – pursue/withdraw, withdraw/pursue. Research shows that men tend to withdraw more frequently, while women tend to pursue. However, in many situations the pattern is reversed. Avoidance and withdrawal are very destructive to relationships and destroy harmony in the home.

The first step you may take to try to prevent avoidance and withdrawal is to realise that you are not independent of one another. Your actions cause reactions and vice versa. You need each other and your family need you both. You will have much more success in dealing with conflict if you work together on it. Gently but firmly, encourage your wife to discuss problems with you. Recovery may be slow and difficult but if you persevere working together, the results will surprise you.

It often happens in a conflict that one person consistently believes that the motives of the other are more negative than is really the case. For example, a woman might say to her husband, "You purposely came home late from work because you knew my mother was visiting. Of course, you don't like my mother anyway", whereas the husband might have genuinely been delayed. Such negative interpretation is very destructive to relationships. It makes conflict and disagreement much harder to deal with. Relationships in homes would be in a sad state if people intentionally did things just to hurt and frustrate others. Fortunately, the number of cases in which this situation occurs is small; more frequently, the actions of one person are interpreted negatively and unfairly. Negative interpretation can be soul-destroying because it is often hard to detect. It can be rooted in and based on the way we form and maintain our beliefs about others. So we must be slow to reach conclusions about the motives for others' actions.

When dealing with negative interpretation, the way to be successful can be to practise *positive thinking*. You should consider that your wife's motives are more positive than you are willing to acknowledge. Ask yourself if you might be negative about her actions. The next suggestion is hard but it is worth a try. Sincerely look for evidence contrary to the negative interpretations you may be inclined to make. For example, if you feel your wife is uncaring, you need to look for evidence to the contrary. Ask yourself, "Does she do things for me that I like? How does she care for the children? How does she cook and look after the home? In what she does, is she trying to improve our relationship?" If you answer these questions honestly, your findings may surprise you and encourage you to be more positive about your wife. Be careful not to play the martyr or feel sorry for yourself. Try to give your wife the benefit of the doubt. Be kind to yourself and do not allow inaccurate interpretations to spoil your efforts and good will.

Speaker–Listener Method

Home is your special place, your sacred space where you enjoy the privilege and the right to live as private people. It is very understandable that you would like to keep your privacy. For you to seek help in dealing with your experience of conflict in your home would indeed be very difficult. It may encourage you to know that there is a method you could use in the privacy of your home that might be of help to you in dealing with your experience of conflict. It is known as the speaker–listener method.[2]

When you use this method you learn to communicate without hurting each other's feelings. It is not a normal way to communicate but it is a relatively safe way to communicate on a difficult issue. In using it you feel safe and it can help bring you closer together. Research, carried out on 3,886 people living together who used this method, proved that 67 per cent of them were better able to handle problems than people who had never attended the sessions.[3] Though initially the process may seem complicated, the practice of it is very simple, and it is this simplicity that gives it such a high success rate. It gives couples the opportunity to communicate when issues are hot and sensitive, or when they are likely to get that way. The method works well because there are certain rules that both of you must follow.

Decide together on a time when you will sit in a quiet room where you are comfortable and won't be disturbed. The general rules of the speaker–listener method are:

- One person in the conflict is the *speaker* and the other person is the *listener*.
- You take your turns in being the *speaker* and the *listener*.
- When you are the *speaker* you are said to "have the floor".
- When you are the *listener* your role is only to listen.

---

[2] An excellent and more detailed account of the speaker–listener technique is given in Markman et al. (2001) *Fighting for Your Marriage: Positive Steps for Preventing Divorce and Preserving a Lasting Love*, San Francisco, CA: Jossey-Bass.

[3] Based on fifteen years of research at the University of Denver, USA.

The person who agrees to speak first is called the speaker. After some time you change roles: the speaker becomes the listener and the listener becomes the speaker. When you use this method your focus is to have good discussions, to learn how to communicate – not to reach conclusions or make decisions. That will come later.

Rules for the Speaker
When you are the speaker, you speak for yourself. Talk about your own feelings, not your perception of the listener's point of view or motives. You must say how you feel personally, for example, "I was upset when you forgot to come home in time to let me go to football practice", not, "You purposely came home late so that I would miss my football practice." It will help if you remember to use "I" statements. When you say, "I was upset", you are expressing your feelings. To say "you purposely forgot" is interpreting the motives of the other person, which may be quite inaccurate. You are not allowed to read the mind of the other person.

You must also use short statements, because the listener has to paraphrase what you have said; for example, "What I understand from what you have said is that you were very upset when I didn't come home in time to let you go to football practice."

If the paraphrase is not accurate, you should politely restate what was not said the way you intended it to be said. In doing so, it is most important to be polite. You must never say something like, "That's not what I said – you've got it all wrong." What you could say is, "I'm sorry if I was not clear, but that is not actually what I said." Remember your goal is to help the listener to hear and understand your point of view.

Rules for the Listener

If you are the listener, the first thing you have to do is to paraphrase what the speaker says. You repeat briefly what you heard the speaker say. You must make sure that you really understand what has been said. If you are not sure, ask the speaker to repeat what was said. You may ask the speaker to clarify but you may not ask questions on any other aspect of the issue.

For example, you must not say things like, "What about all the times you yourself came home late. Does that not matter?" Your role is to listen with your ears and your heart. Never rebut or argue. When the speaker expresses feelings, you must never say, for example, "Sure it's nonsense to feel that way!"

In your role as listener you may not offer an opinion or thoughts. This is the hardest part of being a good listener. As listener, your job is only to listen in the service of understanding the person speaking – to listen attentively, to hear what has been said and to invite the speaker to clarify what you do not understand.

To listen attentively and understand the feelings of the other is a service of love we ought to give each other. Understanding each other's problems is necessary for finding out how to solve our problems.

Finding Solutions – Brainstorming

Let us presume that you have had good discussions during which you have had some success in understanding each other's feelings. You now move on to the next step, which is problem solving. No doubt you have become more aware of many issues of concern. You need to know what are the main issues upon which you must focus your attentions. Problems in a home often seem impossible to surmount but when they are broken down they become more manageable.

You may now wish to look at a process to find solutions to your problems. It is called brainstorming and it can be done in the privacy of your home. It is uncomplicated and easy to manage. It is proven to have worked very well for many couples. If brainstorming is to be effective, you must follow the rules of the game. Arrange a special time when you can sit together, undisturbed, and follow the rules of brainstorming, which are:

- Both of you should make suggestions that you feel would help you to solve your problem. It doesn't matter how crazy the suggestions may sound.

- One of you writes down all the suggestions.
- Do not evaluate the suggestions.
- Do not question or criticise the suggestions either verbally or non-verbally.
- Be light-hearted and enjoy the exercise – you may be as creative as you wish.

One of the great values of brainstorming is that it helps people to think creatively. If you avoid making critical comments on suggestions made, you can encourage each other to come up with all kinds of bright ideas.

Agreement
The brainstorming process can be a wonderful way of finding solutions to problems. When you have written down all your suggestions, study them carefully. Your goal is to come up with a specific solution or a combination of solutions that you both agree to try. It is important to emphasise that the solution is not likely to help unless both of you agree to try it. It is also important to emphasise that the more detailed you are about the solution, the more likely you are to follow it through. It cannot be emphasised enough that there must be a commitment from both of you.

Compromise
It may be easy to see the value of agreement but some people have a problem with *compromise*. To some it sounds more like lose-lose rather than win-win.

Compromise implies giving up part of what we want in order to reach an agreement and for the sake of the relationship. No one gets everything they want. There has to be a little give and take. Two separate individuals may see things differently and might make different decisions. Very often the best solution is a compromise in which neither of you gets everything you wanted. Whatever the agreement and compromise, it is essential that both of you are faithful to what you have agreed to do.

Follow-Up

The difficulty with agreements is that many people fail to keep their commitment to them. This can be very frustrating for those who are anxious to follow through with the agreements. Therefore, it is most important to arrange a time for a follow-up to see how the agreements are working out and to see if any changes are needed to make things work better. Remember the old saying, "If you fail to plan, you plan to fail." This saying carries a lot of wisdom. A follow-up nourishes and encourages accountability. Often we do not get serious about a commitment unless we know there is some point of accountability in the near future. Do not run the risk of spoiling your efforts by not having a follow-up. You owe it to yourselves.

I hope that your honest efforts to give this process a try will help you find a lasting solution to the problem you are experiencing and that your home will be a haven of peace, love and happiness.

Question   Our home is becoming a space for arrivals and departures. It is a place where everyone seems to be in a hurry. The television, the computer and the laptop are given precedence over human contact. There is little or no listening to each other's stories or feelings. Our dog seems to give more attention to each of us by wagging his tail and showing delight at seeing us enter the home. Our meals are rushed and seldom do we sit around the table together as a family. What can we as parents do to humanise our home?

Answer   The Dalai Lama once said, "We humans are social beings. We come into the world as the result of others' actions. We survive here in dependence on others. Whether we like it or not, there is hardly a moment of our lives when we do not benefit from others' activities. So it's hardly surprising that most of our happiness arises in the context of our relationships with others. Nor is it remarkable that our greatest joy should come when we are motivated by concern for others."[4]

Home should be a sacred place where special relationships are made, developed and cherished. These relationships are not possible in a home where people are not really present to each other and are not listening to each other's stories and feelings. The questions for you to ask are: "Why are

---

[4] The Dalai Lama (2002) *The Essence of Wisdom,* London: Abacus, p. 22.

people in my home wanting to leave in such a hurry?" "Why is there such a lack of close human contact?" "What is it that is preventing people in my home from finding a place of rest and comfort where they can form unshakeable, deep and warm relationships?"

Perhaps the answer could be found in the relationship between you as parents. Do you have a sacred time every evening away from the television, computers and mobile phones, where you relate to each other, privately and intimately? Are the other members of the family conscious of this relationship so that a good example is set for all to see? If that relationship is absent, it will not be easy for you to relate to the children, nor will it be easy for the children to relate to you as parents and to each other.

Family meals are a wonderful means of building relationships in the home. How calming, therapeutic, unifying and humanising it is when people sit together at a table and ask God to bless each one and the food they are about to eat. Perhaps the answer to your problem may be to have family meals once or twice a week. But you will need to meet together beforehand to decide when these meals will take place and to get a commitment from all to make it a priority to be present.

Is there something you need to do in your home to help people to relate to each other? For example, could you have a comfortable and attractive room where there is no television, computer or laptop and where people can listen to each other's stories, feeling relaxed and completely at home?

Susan Cuthbert, in her booklet *Home Sweet Home*, states:

> Both imagination and inventiveness, as well as time, money and hard work, are needed to transform an ordinary house or flat into the physical place we long for, a home. But creating an atmosphere of safety, warmth and love, where children can grow and people can lay aside their public masks, demands even more. It takes the best of what we are, not just the tired throwaway leftovers of our hectic workdays. The place that is truly home requires a peaceful spirit, a heart of welcome and that irreplaceable thing, the blessing of God.[5]

---

[5] Susan Cuthbert (ed.) (1999) *Home Sweet Home*, Oxford: Lion Publishing, pp. 3–4.

Question   **My husband appears to be suffering from some form of depression for the past three months. He is losing weight, looks sad and has become irritable in recent times. He won't seek professional help because he says there is nothing wrong with him. The older children and I are extremely worried about him and we don't know what to do. Could you help us?**

Answer   It is common for men, and indeed many depressed people, to think there is nothing wrong with them or to be in denial of their predicament. For many people, seeking help only lowers their self-esteem, reviving memories of being mocked for being emotional, weak or not being independent. It may be that professional help is not the best route in the first instance, as it is possible that your husband would be equally dismissive and in denial with a doctor or a counsellor. The main challenge here is somehow to work with his isolation and despair on a one-to-one basis that allows him to speak about it without fear of rejection, criticism, blame or contempt. This is quite a challenge. It may be that a friend is the best person to undertake this task – for example, his best man or a long-time friend who knows him from way back and with whom he will have less reason to feel ashamed.

Alcohol excess should be avoided because of the risk that, while it will appear to soothe his troubles and help him forget, he will quickly become more depressed, more indulgent and more detached. Often information is helpful rather than advice. Simply finding a leaflet on depression for him, finding a website that relates to depression in men for him to look at or giving him a book where a man with depression describes what happened to him may be sufficient for him to be able to face his difficulties. If you are worried about him you should encourage him to see a professional. However, if you are sufficiently concerned or if he has talked of suicide or being better off dead, do not hesitate to encroach on his boundary walls. He may very well be glad that someone has taken the trouble to do so.

Question   **My wife and I are blessed with four
wonderful children. We are well off
and have a beautiful home. But we
both agree that there is a certain
emptiness in our lives that we cannot
explain. Could it be that we don't pray
at home or worship in Church?**

Answer   Obviously you are fortunate to have a
home like yours, but you feel a certain
emptiness in your home. Many people
are experiencing this sense of emptiness
but they do not express it like you.

Some people have told us that they
are becoming increasingly tired of the
hurly-burly of modern-day living and the
illusion that wealth brings happiness and
is everything. They realise that harmony
and stability in home life are difficult to
maintain in our contemporary society,
despite the fact that we have nicer
homes and lots of modern conven-
iences. These people realise that our
human resources, especially our wealth,
are insufficient to meet the pressures
and challenges of our home life. The
ever-increasing rate of family breakdown
is causing alarm and panic. People are
seeking a solution to this problem other
than through human resources.

The result is that many people like you
experience a pursuit in their hearts for a
transcendent dimension in home life that
will be promoted and enabled to come to
expression through prayer and worship.
Our experience of helping to promote

harmony in homes has shown us that many people are experiencing a certain sense of unease, weariness and boredom at a life that appears to be valueless and without a vision for the future. St Augustine echoed that feeling when he said, "Our hearts are restless until they rest in God."

The well-known rabbi Lionel Blue, renowned author, broadcaster and journalist, in his *Little Book of Blue Thoughts*, says that people talk about God but do not talk to God in prayer. He tells of his young years living in London during World War II. He recalls what his family did first thing in the early mornings: they left the air-raid shelter and checked to see if their home was still standing after an air raid during the night. One morning the home was not there. There was just a big black hole instead. His mother got hold of a barrow and piled whatever was left of the home into it. She wheeled it to the lock-up used by people who had been bombed out. The Rabbi said that he never believed in the permanency of earthly homes ever since. He has realised that his real home is in another dimension and that has saved him much unnecessary pain.[6]

---

[6] Rabbi Lionel Blue (2001) *The Little Book of Blue Thoughts*, London: Rider, pp. 80–1.

Question   In our home we seem to be more and
more tense, edgy and on tenterhooks.
We work hard all day in the family
business and return home so
exhausted that we cannot enjoy our
home comforts. I am afraid that this
situation will get worse and make our
home dysfunctional. Have you any
ideas on how we could address this
problem?

Answer   Contemporary living is getting more and
more stressful. Many people are becom-
ing totally engrossed in striving for
increased wealth and status and the pos-
session of material objects. This obsession with wealth is causing serious levels
of stress. The result is that relationships
in the home are at risk of breaking down.
In some cases homes are becoming like
battlefields, where people cannot find
security, peace, harmony, love and
serenity. People in homes are sometimes merely existing and not fully living.

What can be done to address this
problem? It can help if people become
acutely aware of certain realities through
a process of critical reflection. This critical reflection should focus on questions
such as why do we need to have more
wealth? Is it to have more facilities, more
luxury goods? But what is the use of having more facilities and more luxury goods
if we cannot enjoy them? Would it be better to have less and be more as people,
i.e. to have better relationships, to be

more relaxed and to be in a better position really to enjoy our home comforts. Having more money will not necessarily help us to be happy. Working too hard to gain more money can make us tense and touchy. When we bring all this into our homes it can put relationships at serious risk of breaking down.

You say that you are afraid that the tense situation in your home will get worse and make your home dysfunctional. Perhaps one of the ways to avoid this is for the family to become involved in supporting a worthy cause. Sharing some of the fruits of your hard work with less well-off people could bring satisfaction, joy and a deeper meaning to your life and business.

The obsession with increased wealth often destroys people's sense of good humour. When people are in good humour they tend to be affable and kind to others in their homes. When they are tense and edgy they find it difficult to be cheerful, smile and laugh at the funny side of life. So to make our homes happy and peaceful, people should strive to develop and maintain a sense of good humour in homes.

Question   **The peace and harmony in our home is being disturbed by people who avoid doing some of the necessary chores in the home. These chores are left for one or two people to do. Is there anything you could suggest to solve this problem?**

Answer   Our experience of helping to promote harmony in homes convinces us that tension and discord are experienced because one or two people have to do all necessary chores while others do nothing. This can and does lead to serious difficulties and sometimes a total breakdown of relationships results.

Could we think about this problem? Is there a need to examine the language we use in this matter? The term "doing chores at home" triggers a negative and off-putting reaction. It brings up mental images of doing unattractive and menial tasks, for example cleaning toilets, showers or baths, scrubbing floors and so on. Perhaps a more attractive term like "shared tasks" might create a more positive reaction.

It must be recognised that there is a psychological reluctance in the minds of most people to accept efforts to impose obligations related to home life. There is a real need for a negotiating process with a lot of free-flowing discussion. The discussion will be enriched if an element of self-interest is introduced. This self-interest could be centred around the idea that if all the people living in the home help to do what is necessary, then all will benefit.

Perhaps the following suggestion might help. Someone in the home should call for a get-together to discuss matters related to "shared tasks". The get-together could be in a suitable place, in or out of the home. However, it is important that there be a relaxed and informal social atmosphere.

Psychologically, it would help the discussion and decision-making if the people at the get-together sat side by side, rather than opposite each other. People facing each other tend to respond personally and engage in arguments; people sitting side by side in a semicircle tend to respond to the matter being discussed.

During the session, a facilitator should be selected by the group. Their main task is to keep the meeting on track, to make sure everyone gets a chance to speak and to stimulate discussion by asking questions.

The facilitator should ask the group to list the tasks that have to be done in the home so that the home can be a pleasant and hygienic place to live in. When the list is complete, the facilitator should ask the group to discuss how these tasks could be done in the easiest way and in the shortest possible time. Volunteers are invited from the group to do the tasks. Those who volunteer should be praised for offering their services.

It is very important that a date, time and venue be arranged for a follow-up meeting to assess progress and to fine-tune decisions made at the first meeting.

Question My husband is a wonderful person but tends to be a perfectionist. He expects a lot from our three children and from me. When we do not measure up to his high ideals he becomes upset and disappointed. How can I help him to accept the fact that our children and I are not as perfect as he is?

Answer Perfectionism is difficult because any change of standards to the perfectionist can represent personal failure, which is the thing they fear the most. The perfectionist is trying to create an ideal life, often in defence against some uncontrollable messiness or difficulty during their past. Some people, however, are naturally fussy and tend to be perfectionists, and for many it serves them well in their life. However, if you are not like this, you will find the upset and anger that go with perfectionism difficult to live with and a frequent source of tension and unhappiness in the home.

A head-on approach is unlikely to be helpful, so you need to develop the skills to work with the situation. Relaxation is an important element. The perfectionist will rarely know deep relaxation; if they can be encouraged to discover and pursue it, they will be much less irritated when things are not as they would like them to be. Most perfectionists find relaxation deeply puzzling and are often unable to relax. Perhaps doing relaxation training together will give them the support and reassurance that relaxation can be learned and is transformative in a person's life.

The perfectionist will tend to take over everyone's role and be frustrated that nobody is helping. Having clearly defined roles and responsibilities in the home will be a help. It may be that at times perfectionism has to be indulged, for example in the lead-up to family occasions, visitors, big events and so on, when if everyone doesn't join in and give extra help the tension and irritability will be intolerable. However, there should also be "messy times", when the perfectionist stands back and allows things to be a bit more messy, for example for one day a week or for one week a month, just simply to keep the situation a little fluid.

Severe perfectionism may need professional help both in trying to discover the root of fears that lie behind it, and also help and guidance about not giving in to the impulses to have everything clean, tidy and in order.

Question   There is no harmony or peace in our home because my three-year-old son and I live in constant fear of my partner, who has a violent temper. She slaps my son when he cries or when he does some little thing wrong. When I challenge her about this she threatens to beat me too. What should I do to solve this problem?

Answer   The problem must be causing you and your three-year-old son considerable emotional pain. There is no need for you to continue suffering in this way. Take courage because the law is there to protect you and your son.

Legally, violence to a child or partner is not acceptable in any circumstances. Where a parent is afraid to make a Court application to restrain such behaviour, the help and assistance of the Health Service Executive or other authority should be sought for the protection of the relevant people. The provisions of the Domestic Violence Act, 1996, would apply to the circumstances outlined in this case. It is also open to the applicant to leave the home if the situation becomes intolerable, and to apply to the Court for the necessary reliefs.

It is most important for you to protect your well-being and that of your three-year-old son. For that reason it is advisable for you to talk over the problem with your family doctor, who may, if necessary, make arrangements for you to see a counsellor and for your son to be referred to a child clinic. This should be done as a matter of urgency.

Question **My husband demands unreasonable accounts of my movements and my social contacts, including contacts with my family. He shouts at me a lot and I am afraid that one day he will hit me or our children. What should I do? How can I help him to overcome this aggressive mood?**

Answer It is understandable that you feel fearful for yourself and your children when your husband shouts at you. The fear of him striking your children and you must cause you much pain. Perhaps you should consider some of the following ideas.

From what you have said about your husband, it would seem that he is a bully. It is important that you should not feel you are at fault and you should avoid any feelings of self-blame.

When he shouts, it is advisable to lower your tone of voice and speak very slowly and in a determined way. This may make him realise that shouting gets him nowhere. The wrong thing for you to do would be to shout back at him. That will get you nowhere.

At a deeper level, perhaps it might be good for you to ask yourself what triggers his aggressive mood. Is it something you say or do? Could you avoid saying and doing those things?

Your husband's shouting is probably the presenting problem, i.e. the symptom of something else. You have to reflect on the question: what is the real problem, i.e. the latent problem, the underlying difficulty? Maybe he is shouting because he thinks – incorrectly – that he will only be listened to if he shouts. Or perhaps he feels that no one is listening to his feelings and he believes if he shouts it will solve the problem.

He may shout because he feels frustrated. He might believe that his emotional and psychological needs are not being attended to in his home. He may think that you are neglecting him because you are too engrossed with the children.

It could help to solve the problem if you praise him for the good things he does in and out of the home. He may have a poor self-image and believe that he is a failure as a husband and a father. Then out of frustration at his perceived failure, he shouts at you. You can help him by praising what he does well in and out of the home.

Perhaps the cause of his aggressive mood is related to his workplace. Is there insecurity about his job? Is it shaky because of some downsizing that is going on? Perhaps he finds the rapid pace of technological change difficult to handle.

Intimate relationships inevitably involve some antagonism as well as love. However, if that antagonism results in out-of-control behaviour such as physical violence, then very serious action has to be taken to protect your children and yourself. That may mean recourse to the courts to obtain a Barring Order. But everything else should be tried before taking such drastic actions, including intimate dialogue with your husband when both of you are feeling calm and loving. Perhaps at those times you could say something like this to him: "You know I love you and you know how worried I am when you are not feeling good. But I become *very* worried when you shout at me because I fear it might lead to even more upset and possibly injury. Can you help me to be less worried?" This kind of statement, known as the "I" statement, does not put any blame on him and may encourage him to talk about how he really feels.

If the situation with your husband persists or gets worse, you must consider taking more determined action by confronting him. However, before you confront him it is vital that you build up your inner strength. This can be done by improving your social life, speaking to trusted friends and, if necessary, talking to your family doctor, who may arrange for you to see a counsellor.

It is important to keep a detailed diary of all the aggressive actions of your husband. The details should include dates, times, places and how you felt as a result of the aggressive behaviour.

When you confront your husband, you should talk about his aggressive behaviour and not about him as a person. It is important that you do not allow your husband to see that you are afraid. Bullies love weakness and they tend to exploit it.

You must not lose your temper when you are confronting him and say things you might later regret. Above all, you must not use hurtful language because it would make things worse.

If the confrontation fails to show good results, it might help if you could encourage your husband to visit the family doctor, who may advise him to have professional counselling.

Remember, if your husband is ever physically violent towards you or your children, you should call the Gardaí immediately. It may be possible to obtain a Barring Order to prevent your husband coming within a certain distance of you and the children.

Question   **My husband and I realise that our parents and grandparents passed on to us deep spiritual values and taught us how to maintain and develop these values. But now we realise that we are failing to pass on these values to our children. We are shy to talk about them to our children or to introduce prayer in our home. Have you any suggestions as to how we could address this issue?**

Answer   It would be good for you to realise that you are passing on values to your children by the way you are living your lives in the home. Children learn more by example than words. However, something more is needed. It is necessary for the proper formation of the children and for their future lives to speak about these values and to teach them their importance. Values such as truth, honesty, justice, love, concern, sharing and so on need to be discussed and taught to the children.

Prayer can be helpful in maintaining and nurturing these values. Therefore, there would seem to be no reason for you to feel shy about introducing prayer into your home and this should be done at an early age so that prayer becomes an integral part of family life. Children are attracted to informal and spontaneous prayer that relates to values in their lives and their natural love of creativity.

The "hands game" is one of the creative ways of helping to pass on values and assisting the whole family to pray.

The game is simple. Each one in the family is given two sheets of paper and is asked to draw the shape of their hand on each sheet. On one sheet of paper, they are asked to write five things (one on each finger) that help to make people good. On the other sheet of paper, they are asked to write five things (one on each finger) that prevent people from being good. Then they discuss what they have written. After the discussion the family pray together, asking God for courage to do those things that make people good.

Question   **My partner and I have two children, aged twelve and fourteen. Because we have a limited income we have to make an annual budget and implement it. Our children seem to think that we have unlimited resources and they look for more and more pocket money and luxury items. When we tell them that we do not have money for these things they do not believe us or they say we do not love them. The result is a lack of peace in our home. Can you make any suggestions to solve this problem?**

Answer   Usually children of twelve or fourteen respond in a more positive way when they are participants and not observers of an activity or process. Children of that age love to be consulted, to listen and to participate in making plans and being part of "the action". For that reason, you should invite your children to give their views on how to make a family budget with you. If they are not involved in making the budget, they will continue to make unreasonable demands. You should make it clear to them how much you love and care for them; tell them that it would be a great source of joy for you if you had the money to meet all their demands, but that the money is not available.

To convince them of this, you need to tell them what your income is and what it costs to pay medical bills, food, clothing, heating, school fees, school books, insurance, pocket money and so on. You must encourage them to be understanding and supportive as you make the budget together as a family.

Question   I'm very concerned about my eight-year-old son who is very good at studies and is very handsome. He is being bullied very badly at school. Some of the other boys call him names, push him about and steal his lunch. They demand money from him and say that if he does not pay them they will give him a beating. He is losing weight, wets the bed, hates going to school and seems to be always sad. My husband seems to lack compassion for his son and says he must face the real world and learn how to defend himself. What should I do to address this problem?

Answer   Without any doubt, what is happening to your son is a serious form of bullying. That is evident from the definition of bullying given by the Department of Education and Science in its *Guidelines on Countering Bullying in Primary and Post-Primary School* (1993). The guidelines define bullying as "the repeated aggression, verbal, psychological or physical, conducted by an individual or a group against others". The effects of this sad experience on your son are typical of people who are being bullied.

Your son would benefit from being told that the fault is with the bullies, not with him. He is the innocent one and does not deserve to be bullied. Help him to build up his self-confidence. Encourage him to be assertive. He should not let the bullies know that he is upset. Tell him to keep his head and shoulders up and not to look down. Advise him not to believe what the bullies might say about him. Encourage him to relate to a few trusted friends in the school and outside it. Motivate him to get involved in school activities. Advise him to make eye contact with the bullies, stare them in the face for a few seconds and then protest loudly when they bully him. He should shout in a strong voice, "Get away and leave me alone!" This will attract the attention of those in authority. Tell him never to retaliate physically because that will give the bullies an excuse to continue their behaviour and call it self-defence.

Doing a role-play with him might help him. Let him play the bully and you play him. Then reverse the roles.

Your son needs a lot of love and support at this time, from you and your husband. Both of you must reassure him that you are aware of his deep pain and you must convince him that you are there to protect and care for him. You need to be vigilant because of the possibility of depression. If your son continues to be upset, you should consult your family doctor.

You and your husband should work together to solve this problem. Your husband probably loves his son dearly. He must realise that the boy needs his compassion and it is not helpful to suggest that his son must face the real world and learn how to defend himself. His son needs his father to help him to defend himself, but using physical means is not the best way to do this.

You, with your son's help, must keep a written and detailed record of all the bullying incidents suffered by him. Make sure not to exaggerate the accounts of the incidents. The record should give dates, times and places where the bullying happened. The names of all the bullies involved and who were present should be noted. The record should state how your son felt when he was bullied.[7]

You would be well advised to make contact with the head of the school by telephone or by letter. Do not go to the school in person because that could put pressure on your son. He may be afraid of being called a "rat" or of what his classmates would think and do as a reaction. Perhaps you could ask the head of the school to let you have an appointment in private when the school children have gone home. Please be aware that school staff usually take bullying issues very seriously. They need people like you to help them make their school bully-free. You should also remember that the majority of teachers are under pressure today and often find

---

[7] Tony Byrne, Kathleen Maguire and Brendan Byrne (2004) *Bullying in the Workplace, Home and School: Questions and Answers*, Dublin: Blackhall Publishing.

it difficult to deal with children who are unruly and who bully others.

Schools have an obligation to investigate complaints about bullying. However, if you are unhappy about the school's response or if the school has no formal procedure in place to investigate your complaint, you might consider contacting the school's board of management for assistance or seek advice from the parents' association, if the school has one.

Question   **Our children of five, eight and ten seem to be showing signs of becoming real bullies when they grow up. They tend to bully each other and their friends. I do not know what is making them act this way and I do not know what my husband and I can do to let them see that this is not a good way of acting. Can you help us to solve this problem?**

Answer   You must take steps to encourage your children to stop bullying. But first make sure that what they are doing is really bullying, which is defined as the repeated inappropriate behaviour, direct or indirect, verbal, physical or psychological, conducted by one or more persons against another or others. Name-calling, slagging, teasing and banter will always go on where children of five, eight and ten live together in a home. However, when a line is crossed, it can be devastating for the child affected by it. The age-old excuse "we were only messing" needs to be challenged constantly in homes. The behaviour becomes bullying when the same person or persons are repeatedly on the receiving end of negative attention, against their wishes, and are unable to prevent it.

If you are convinced that your children's actions with each other and their friends are indeed bullying, you must encourage them to stop bullying. Perhaps it would be helpful to consider some of the following suggestions.

When you see one of your children bullying you must act quickly, particularly if the target of the bullying is smaller and could be in danger of being hurt. You should remember when children are bullying they are usually in a heightened emotional state and can act in a very dangerous way. So you should separate the bully from the one who is being bullied. Explain very clearly to the bully that the behaviour you have witnessed is wrong and unacceptable.

It is important to calm down the children when you find them bullying and calm down anyone who may be upset. When you have done this, listen to both sides to determine what actually happened. Most children in a situation like this need a cooling-off time – even a few minutes will help. Sit with the child who has been bullying and let them see that they are responsible for the aggressive actions. You must try to get them to accept this. Help this child to identify the cause of their bullying. You may have to ask questions such as, "I think you pushed your sister and called her bad names because you wanted to take her jigsaw. Did you try asking her for a loan of it?" The child will need help in understanding their behaviour. Try to explain to the child that everyone gets upset sometimes and that there are easier and better ways to solve problems. Tell the child that people cannot always get what they want. It may be difficult but you must get the child to apologise to the child they have bullied. If they are reluctant to do so, wait until they have calmed down and are less angry.

Children sometimes act aggressively in public or when there are visitors in the house. They think they will get away with it because you won't correct them at that time. You may be embarrassed by their aggressive behaviour in this situation and you may feel like covering up their bad behaviour but you should correct the child quietly on the spot. The aggressive child will learn not to take advantage of you in public or in front of visitors to your home. Do not worry about other parents who may be looking on – they will understand.

It is most important for you to acknowledge the good behaviour of children who tend to bully others, whether it is a room well tidied, a game well played or an honest effort to improve behaviour at home.

If you notice that one of your children continues to bully and if their aggressive behaviour gets worse, it may be necessary for you to ask advice from a doctor or child psychiatrist.

Some researchers believe that children who do not receive sufficient love and affection from their parents or who are criticised unduly may be prone to aggressive behaviour. Another theory is that children who observe aggressive behaviour in their parents and other adults at home tend to identify with this behaviour and imitate it. Other researchers believe that bullying attitudes are acquired in children who are continuously controlled by parents. If no reason is given to the children for stopping their aggressive behaviour, a little battle ensues between the parents and the children. Because of parent power, the children will usually lose the battle. Then, when the parental control is absent, the children can decide to win their battle and engage in bullying behaviour.

Question   **My sixteen-year-old son has a bad temper. If my husband and I do not give him what he wants he throws things around the home, bangs doors and curses. I don't know what to do. He is a strong lad and I fear for myself, my husband and the other children. Please advise me what should be done to deal with this problem.**

Answer   Angry outbursts in teenagers are common, a part of normal development but no less difficult to cope with. Being sixteen is not easy and frustration, confusion, anger and insecurity are ever present. By and large, a person will work their way through this in due course and it won't continue indefinitely.

However, in the meantime it is important to set limits because of the impact of this behaviour on other family members. It will be more difficult if you have had trouble setting limits up to now. Equally, *both* parents or family elders must be resolved to work together toward addressing the issues. Otherwise you will increase the confusion and provide opportunities for disagreement and manipulation.

It is important to stay within your own limits in addressing displays of temper. Not raising your own voice, keeping a cool head, taking time out and not giving up are crucial. Remember that the word "parent" means control and it is vital for a parent to understand that they must assert and maintain the absolute right to exercise this control in the home. Giving in is the worst option of all.

Sit down and discuss with your son what he thinks of his own behaviour. This may not be very fruitful: he may acknowledge some unacceptability but blame someone else. Negotiate a set of rules that he will sign up to. Make agreements about what will happen if the rules are kept and what will happen if the rules are broken. You *must* follow through on this. Have regular, at least weekly, meetings to review the situation, but these meetings should be pleasant and linked to something he deserves, such as a nice meal or pocket money or whatever. Be absolutely explicit that violence is not permitted and, if it is occurring, represents a grave threat to family safety. Again, asserting your parental authority is crucial.

Irritability and temper outbursts commonly follow withdrawal or recovery from drug or alcohol indulgence. If this is a factor, limiting access to money and other privileges must be undertaken. One-to-one time with a parent is very valuable and happens much less often than you would think. Going for a cycle with dad, to a film with mum or to a football match with granddad will be an important neutralising and bonding alternative. Similarly, physical exercise of any kind will defuse frustration and anger and improve mood.

Your son will need support and encouragement as well as friends to ensure that this happens. If things are getting worse or an assault has occurred, the Juvenile Liaison Officer of the Gardaí is an important ally. Do not shirk from demonstrating that domestic violence is completely unacceptable. If you do, you will have created a bully who will never be a mature adult.

Question   **My seventeen-year-old adopted son has always known he was adopted from an early age. We've had a loving and close relationship all along, but lately he is distant and aloof. He has become more overtly challenging of our family values, but when asked indicates that he has no issue with adoption. I do know, however, that he would like to meet his biological mother, even though he hasn't told us this. What should we do?**

Answer   It is quite common for adoptive children to go through something like this. Issues of belonging and identity are particularly important during the teenage years; even though he has a secure sense of belonging and a clear identity as a member of your family, he will have deeper questions about his adoption that often only emerge at this time. He may be reluctant to discuss these with you for fear of somehow causing offence or showing lack of gratitude. His attempts to contact his biological mother are easier and are often well facilitated and advised by the adoption agencies.

It is quite common for adoptive parents to be somewhat puzzled and upset, feeling powerless in the situation to know what to do. It may be some time before he can actually fully discuss his feelings in the open with you because he needs to work them out in his own head first and foremost. You will find that the adoption agency has a social worker who can advise him individually on the issues of contacting and meeting his biological mother, if this is possible. The adoption agencies are familiar with and skilled in dealing with the issues that this brings up.

In the meantime it's best that you signal your continued support and love for him but do so in a way that allows him to exercise and show some distance at the same time. It's best not to over-exert or encroach upon his natural distancing process, which in time may well work out in a way that both he and you will be closer at the end of it. Any feelings of hurt or upset on your part are understandable, but shouldn't intrude in the relationship. He will already sense this and will probably go to some lengths to spare you as much of this as possible. It's important not to let a rift develop at this time and that the other family members make allowances accordingly. The feelings of his siblings could be quite heated as well and they may feel aggrieved at this late intrusion into family harmony. They should be counselled in a way that allows them to articulate these feelings, but in a way that doesn't inflame any hurt or anger.

You will probably find that it will take at least a couple of years for him to figure out his feelings about being adopted and you need to work within this kind of time frame. Most adopted children expand their identity to include both their adoptive and biological parentage at the end of this process, often in very creative and inspiring ways. However, you won't be privy during this to his intimate feelings, which he may not even be able to face himself, except slowly and painfully in some cases, and he may even mourn now what has been lost many years before. Fruitless soul-searching about whether you did things the right or the wrong way won't help, as you need to unite as a couple and be confident that what happened was the right thing and what the outcome will be will also be the right thing. The adoption agency may also be able to assist you in regard to your own strategy during this time. It's worth remembering that while love conquers all, it needs to accommodate distance, difference and uncertainty along the way.

Question My twenty-year-old son looks very strained at times. He says he does not sleep well in the early hours of the morning when he returns from work. Very often he is intoxicated when he comes home. I am not sure, but I think he may be using drugs. He seems to have mood swings and when he feels down he talks about ending his life. This situation is disturbing the harmony in our home. My wife and I are very worried. Can you help us to know what we should do about this problem?

Answer No doubt this must be a great source of worry for you and your wife. Your son urgently needs your loving support and, above all, he needs professional help. From what you say about him, it sounds as if he may be suicidal. When he says he wants to end his life, you must take him seriously. Do not presume he is trying to upset you. Above all do not argue with him. Avoid saying things such as, "Now son, you don't really mean that." "Do not worry – everyone feels bad at times." "It will pass." "Remember you are better off than most lads your age." "You have a great job and a good home." Those kinds of statements are not helpful. The worst thing you can do is to show an aloof and uncaring attitude.

Praise him for having the courage to share his feelings with you. Tell him that you know it takes a lot of courage to say that he feels like killing himself. Tell him that you are there for him and that you love him as he is. Tell him that he could have a great future. All these kinds of statements will give him a sense of hope. You should make him feel that you are listening to him actively, that is, listening to his words and feelings. To do that, you could say to him, "Tell me about yourself and how you are really feeling. I am here for you. When did you first feel bad?" Encourage him to analyse his problem. Keep him talking and, if he cries, tell him that it is good to do so. It will help him. Give him all the time he needs. Assure him that whatever is wrong with him can be addressed. Encourage him to see the family doctor by saying to him that it may be good for him to get a tonic from the doctor because he is working too hard. It would be wise for you to have a confidential word with the doctor before your son's visit to explain that your son is showing suicidal tendencies. The doctor may arrange professional counselling for him or have him assessed by a mental health professional.

If your son refuses to go to the doctor, ask his friends to help you to convince him to do so. If he has a partner, they might convince him to seek professional help.

If your son shows a sudden change in his behaviour and appears to be recovering, you should know that this may be a time when he is very vulnerable and at high risk. You should pay more attention to him than ever before. Do not leave him alone if at all possible. Remove sharp knives, ropes and tablets or anything obvious he could use in your home to end his life.

You must remember that your son needs professional help and if he gets it he may recover. Your loving support will help him immensely to get better. But you have to keep strong and care for yourselves during these difficult times. If you are a religious person you will know the power of prayer and what it can do to help your son.

Question   Our two young adults live in our home
and at times can disrupt the peace
and harmony by their behaviour. They
are reluctant to pay for their upkeep,
even though they earn good money.
They don't seem to have any plans for
finding their own accommodation.
Being their parents, we don't wish to
ask them to move out but we feel that
they are exploiting our home and that
they should have their own homes.
We want to have space to ourselves
and have peace in our advancing
years. What should we do?

Answer   It sounds like your two young adults are
only adult in years but rather adolescent
in their maturity. However, they are in
good company, as many parents
increasingly report a situation like this
where the overfed chicks are reluctant to
leave the nest. Unless they have to, they
won't, and they will displace you and
regard the nest as their own.

It is time to get real and get them out
of the nest. You have got to move
beyond being the parent of an adolescent to being the parent of an adult. You
need to realise that you cannot protect
and patrol their lives to the degree that
you needed to when they were adoles-
cents, despite the many fears and haz-
ards that you can see out there. Unless
they make their own mistakes and have
their own regrets, they will never become
mature adults.

It would be wise to arrange a chat with them. It might be good to have it in a place and at a time of their choice, preferably outside the home and in a relaxing venue. During the session you should gently suggest that it would be good if they considered the possibility of having their own accommodation. You might tell them that you would be willing to give them a little help in setting up their accommodation. Ask them to set a target for moving out of your home. Emphasise that they will have more independence and privacy in their own place of living. They will be free to invite their friends at any time of the day or night. Tell them that they will always be welcome to visit your home and have a bite to eat.

When they leave, you should not pay their bills, bail them out financially, be responsible for their lifestyle purchases or launder their clothes, as to do so would hinder the process of maturing.

Question   **Eighteen months ago our ten-year-old son was killed in a freak accident. Since then life for me, my husband and our twelve-year-old daughter has been very difficult. We are tense and irritable with each other. We don't socialise any more. Our daughter, who was of a very happy disposition, has become quiet and often looks very sad. I feel desperate. Sometimes I feel I am going crazy. Is there anything we can do to bring peace and happiness back into our home?**

Answer   The parting with a loved one by death is probably the most painful experience you will ever have to bear. It has been rated as the most stressful of all the life-changing situations. No wonder then that you feel so devastated by the sudden loss of your son. It is as though part of your own life has been taken from you.

Your husband and your daughter are also grieving, each in their own special way. Grieving is very individual. It would help greatly if each of you knew and understood, as best you could, something of how the other is hurting.

For a moment, consider how your husband may be feeling. No doubt he is suffering the deep pain of loneliness and loss. Unfortunately, some men seem to have great difficulty in sharing their feelings. They hide their emotions for fear of appearing weak, seeing tears as a sign of weakness. Perhaps your husband is just not able to talk about his feelings. It is quite possible that he is so overcome with grief that he is not able to do what deep down in his heart he would love to do – reach out to you. He may be so uncomfortable with his grief that he is afraid to talk in case he says something that would upset you.

Your daughter, too, is hurting. Children experience grief just as we adults do but most children do not have the words to tell us about their feelings. If we try to over-protect or shelter children from experiencing grief they can turn to their imagination, which often produces a worse situation than the real one. Young people often assume they are somehow to blame. Children may interpret their parents' silence and sadness as a sign that they are disappointed with them. Because you are so upset at the loss of your son, your daughter may feel that you loved him more or that he was more important to you than she is. These may be some of the sentiments your daughter is experiencing. One thing is sure: she is struggling to cope with the loss of her brother. Because she sees you and her dad quiet and sad, she may be afraid to talk in case she would cause you further upset or she may feel you would be annoyed with her.

During this difficult time, it is very important for you to take care of yourself. It can be much harder to watch those we love suffer than experience our own pain. If you want to help the others through their grief and restore peace to your home, you must begin with yourself. By requesting help, you have taken your first step on the road to recovery. This road will have many twists and turns, but you will reach the end and your life will improve. Be patient with yourself – there is no time limit on grief. Take each day gently – each hour, each moment, each feeling – and you will begin to encounter the power of healing in your heart and in your home.

It may help you to cope with the emotions of grief if you reflect briefly on the following thoughts.

Shock and Denial
On hearing the news of the death of a loved one, we are shocked, stunned, overwhelmed. The shock may be so intense that we can forget the details of what has happened. It shuts down our emotional system. It could be considered as God's and the mind's way of providing a cushion to protect us from the full impact of our loss until we are able to cope with the reality of the death.

Anger
Anger is another very natural phase of grieving. Anger can be directed at anyone – the doctor, the nurse, a family member, even at God. Anger is a feeling very commonly expressed by children. It can be a sign of frustration, and the less

able people are to express it, the angrier they can become.

Guilt
Feelings of guilt are particularly painful. The bereaved think of the many things they could have done but didn't do. They want another chance to make amends and it is not there for them. This is a period of "if onlys" – "If only I had ..." It must be stressed that there are two kinds of guilt:

- *Realistic guilt* is the guilt we feel when we have done something deliberately to hurt the loved one. This guilt becomes more painful when the person dies before we have a chance to say we are sorry.
- *Unrealistic guilt* is the guilt we feel when we do something in all good faith; at the time we did what we believed was best and now that our loved one is dead we feel we could have done more.

Guilt, whether real or unreal, is very painful.

Depression
It is one thing to feel sad and lonely when someone dies but some people can suffer deep depression to the point of despair and desperation. At this time, some people may even feel suicidal. We may think we are going crazy. It is important to know that all these feelings are the normal emotions of grieving. After a death, children may become clinically

depressed, particularly if they have not been able to grieve.

Physical Distress
Grief can also affect us physically. We may experience severe headaches, tiredness, insomnia, chest pains or chest tightness. We may not be able to eat or we may eat excessively.

Loss and Loneliness
As time goes on we may become more aware of the reality of death. There is the empty chair, the empty bed, the voice that's never heard and the footsteps that never arrive. At this time, some people seek help because they are looking for a quick solution for the pain, while others prefer to wait in the hope it will all go away. It is an extremely painful and lonely experience.

Withdrawal
The bereaved often withdraw from all relationships and social activities. This is a sort of safety measure, a way of avoiding the reality and the fear of having to answer over and over again questions such as, "How are you?" Just like shock and denial, withdrawal helps us to cope until we are able to deal with the reality of our loved one's death.

Acceptance
The bereaved often say, "This is all too much. It will never end." But you can be

assured that the pain *will* end. This is very hard to believe when you are in the depths of grief. It will ease – at least it will lose its intensity. The pain may recur periodically, even for a number of years. Feelings will come and go. Some days we will feel good and other days we will feel bad. It is encouraging to know that each experience faced and dealt with brings us another step in the right direction – a step towards recovery.

Accepting the reality of our loved one's death is very difficult but it is only through acceptance that healing can take place. Some people can feel guilty at the idea of acceptance. Here, acceptance means the realisation that we are unable to change what has happened, that life has to go on, that our deceased loved one would want us to be happy, that we have other people in our lives who love us and who need to be loved by us. If you can come to this realisation, you will experience having a new energy and enthusiasm for life. You will find a new sense of self-worth, a new calmness within you. Little things won't irritate you as much. You will take yourself less seriously and you will be able to laugh once more.

To reach this stage of acceptance, you need others. You cannot do it alone. Share your feelings and emotions with someone. Talk to someone you trust and with whom you feel safe. You may need to talk to your family doctor or a professional counsellor. You are probably the best judge of whom you should talk to and when to do so, because it is very important for you to feel comfortable and safe when sharing your feelings.

Perhaps you believe your best starting point is to share your thoughts and feelings with your husband. Perhaps such an initiative on your part is just what he is waiting for – it could trigger the reopening of communication between you. Talk to him about your pain, your feelings. Encourage him to share his feelings with you. Do not be afraid to talk about your son and how you both miss him. Share your worries about your daughter and what you can do together to help her through her grief.

Try the same with your daughter. She needs your love and the reassurance of your love and care for her. Talk to her about your son and try to get her to talk about him. Allow her to cry and do not be afraid to cry with her. It will help her to understand that it is all right to cry, that it will help her to recover. Respect her need to be alone, to be quiet and sad, even though it might upset you. She will come to realise that you and your husband love her and she will begin to feel secure again. Somewhere down the line she too will once again be able to laugh.

Sharing your thoughts and feelings with your husband, and both of you coming together for your daughter, will, hopefully, be the key to your recovery. If you work together, there is no reason why you should not experience the peace and happiness you enjoyed before the death of your son. You will find that you are stronger people than you ever were before. Of course, you will never forget your son. A wise man once said, "Our departed loved ones die only when they are forgotten." Your son will live on in your loving memories of him and your home will again be a haven of love, peace and harmony.

Question   My mother lives in my home. My husband and I try to rear our children in
the best way possible but my mother
tends to come between us and our
children. She tends to spoil them.
They run to her for comfort when we
correct them. This causes tension in
our home. My mother is almost sev-
enty years of age and our children are
twelve and fourteen years. My husband and I are feeling the strain of my
mother's interference. What can we
do to maintain harmony in our home?

Answer   The responsibility of rearing children is
not an easy task at any time. If a grand-
parent interferes in the process, that task
can become extremely difficult. When
you achieve motherhood you have
become an independent and fully
autonomous adult, which both you and
your mother need to acknowledge.

It may be you both have never actually
thought about or allowed yourselves to
realise this. Your mother will act like your
mother until she realises that she does
not need to do so. Therefore, you need
to stop acting like her child and assert
more authority and autonomy in your
home. You must become empowered by
your own motherhood rather than disem-
powering her of hers. She will then relate
to you more as an equal adult, who will
offer advice when it is sought, rather than
interfering. It may be that your relationship has been such that you feel inse-

cure and inadequate in regard to her. She may have contributed to this. You need to work this out and get over it.

Your husband should privately support you rather than openly confront or challenge your mother. His role is to help you evolve into the fully empowered person you need to become. Similarly, your children will relate more directly to you when you assume this new role.

Your mother will be better able to relinquish her power base when she sees your own empowerment, and she will respect and learn not to challenge your authority in your own home.

Question   **My husband and I are experiencing some difficulties. He claims that I give preferential hospitality to my parents and in-laws when they visit our home. He says that I do not give the same hospitality to his parents and in-laws when they visit the home. I don't intend to discriminate in this way, but I don't have a very good relationship with his family. What do you think I should do to solve the problem, which is becoming a source of tension and disharmony between us?**

Answer   Difficult relationships with in-laws can be very unpleasant. They can cause painful misunderstandings. It is vital that you address the problem before it escalates into a serious situation.

You admit that you do not have a good relationship with your husband's family. So even though you do not intend to discriminate in any way, it might be that you unknowingly display your feelings. Are you sure of your husband's relationship with your family? Could it be that his relationship with your family is also not good? Perhaps it would help if you and your husband would agree to a quiet and open talk about this. It is most important to understand each other's feelings.

You might like to use a simple technique that has proved to be very successful in solving problems like yours. It's not complicated and both of you could have fun with it.

You and your husband each take a sheet of paper. Do not let each other see what you have written on this paper until the exercise is complete. You and your husband should think about your families for a few moments. Then you write four good qualities of your husband's family and your husband writes four good qualities of your family. After that you write four good qualities of your own family and your husband writes four good qualities of his family.

Now the fun starts. You read to each other what you have written. Compare the similarities and the differences.

The final step in the technique is for you to write four ways in which you could make your husband's family welcome in your home. Your husband writes down four ways in which he could make your family welcome. Then you read to each other what you have written.

There is a beautiful Hawaiian prayer that is worth noting. It says, "All powerful Creator, make the roof on my home wide enough for all opinions. Oil the door of my home so it opens easily to relatives, friends and strangers. Set such a table in my home that my whole family may speak kindly and freely around it."

Question   **My sister and I live together in the same home and we also work together in our own business. For many years we have enjoyed harmony both at home and at work. However, in the last year we are experiencing serious relationship problems. Do you think that professional mediation might help us to resolve our differences?**

Answer   This is a particularly painful problem for you and your sister because it affects both your home life and workplace. It is wise of you to consider professional mediation, which facilitates people like you who are having difficulties, to find a way forward to which they can both agree. The professional mediator works with those in dispute to enable them to hear each other's needs and find a way to meet these needs rather than prove who is right and who is wrong. We tend to become adversarial when we argue, and adversarial processes do not create good relationships. Mediation can provide healing for some, mend differences for others and enable continued involvement between people who need to work and/or live together. Sometimes mediation simply allows people to find ways forward to end a personal relationship but allows a business relationship to continue.

Family businesses can be very successful but also fraught with the difficulties of family dynamics. If you and your sister decide to go to mediation, you can decide between you what you want from your relationship, and work towards this through the mediation process.[8]

---

[8] The Conflict Resolution and Mediation Consultants can be contacted at crmc@eircom.net or telephone (01) 2789897.

REFLECTIONS

Cicero made a wise statement when he said, "a life without reflection is a life not worth living". We all need quiet moments that help us to get in touch with our inner selves. We would like to suggest that you spend a little time reading the following reflections in a quiet space, with lighted candles and soft music. Hopefully, during this time you will be able to explore ways of promoting harmony and peace in your home.

We do not suggest that these reflections will be suitable for everyone. However, we are convinced of the relevance and usefulness of the reflections because of the written evaluations made by the five thousand or so people who have attended our seminars and courses. The majority of these people stated that they found the reflections to be very therapeutic, illuminating and helpful in seeing the realities of their lives.

REFLECTION

I need a place that I can call home: a place to rest, regroup and ready myself for the outside world again.

Something deep within me yearns for that place of security and comfort, where others know my history and I know theirs.

Both imagination and inventiveness, as well as time, money and hard work, are needed to transform a house into that sacred place I call home. But creating an atmosphere of safety, warmth and love, where all can grow and people can lay aside their public masks, demands even more.

Home takes the best of me, not just the tired, throw-away leftovers of my hectic workdays. The place that is truly home requires a peaceable spirit, a heart of welcome and that irreplaceable thing we call love.

Silent reflection

Prayer

All-powerful Creator, make the roof of my home wide enough for all opinions. Oil the door of my home so it opens easily to friends and strangers, and set such a table in my home that all within and all who come there may speak kindly and freely around it.

REFLECTION

My home should be a place where I can throw my cares aside as my mind puts down its burden from the labour of the day.

    My home should be a sacred space where I can enjoy the rest I have longed for all day and where I can experience the gift of inner peace and harmony.

Silent reflection

Prayer

God of compassion, love and peace, help me to know how I can improve the quality of my home life, both for myself and all those who live with me. Help everyone in my home to listen to the views, opinions and beliefs of others. Help me to appreciate the good qualities of everyone in my home and be willing to praise them for these good qualities.

REFLECTION

My home cannot be a sacred place of peace and harmony if I disrespect the rights of others and think of my rights only.

My home cannot be a haven of love and warmth if I do not forgive others who have offended me at home.

My home cannot be a place where everyone feels respected and accepted if I do not make myself available to those who need my support and compassion.

My home cannot be a place of comfort and security if I do not treat others as I would like them to treat me.

Silent reflection

Prayer

Loving Creator, I ask you to help all who live in my home to act more justly and to love more tenderly so that all of us in my home may enjoy peace and harmony.

REFLECTION

No one has a right to take away my God-given dignity in my home.

I have a right to enjoy peace, love, serenity and harmony in that sacred space I call home.

But I have an obligation to help all those who live in my home to enjoy good relationships with me and each other.

Silent reflection

Prayer

Lord help me to find a way of promoting peace, harmony, love and serenity in my home. Inspire me and all those who live with me to respect our inner feelings, opinions and differences. Lord, when we disagree and have conflict help us to respond in a way that will not destroy but will deepen our relationships with each other.

REFLECTION

The perfect person does not exist in this world of ours.
Neither does such a person exist in our home.
If we accept this reality, it will be easier for us to live
in peace and harmony.

Silent reflection

Prayer

**Loving Creator, help us in our home to accept
our differences and our imperfections
with respect and tolerance. Encourage us to
appreciate our good qualities and be grateful
for them. Bless our home with an abundance
of peace, love and joy.**

REFLECTION

My home is just like a mirror.

If I look into the mirror of my home with love, it reflects it back.

If look into the mirror of my home with forgiveness, it reflects it back.

If I look into the mirror of my home with trust, it reflects it back.

Silent reflection

Prayer

Lord, help me to bring a spirit of love, forgiveness and trust into my home. Teach me to be generous in serving those with whom I live. Help me to realise that in giving I receive and that the more happiness I give to others in my home, the more I will have for myself.

APPENDIX

SUPPORT ORGANISATIONS
A number of organisations offer support and advice to those striving for harmony in the home. Here is a selection of these organisations.

The *Support for Families Directory* is published by the Family Support Agency. It contains the names, addresses and telephone numbers of a wide variety of support groups and counselling services throughout the Republic of Ireland. **The Family Support Agency**: St Stephen's Green House, Earlsfort Terrace, Dublin 2. Tel: (01) 6114100

Accord: Marriage Counselling Service
Tel: Central office (01) 5053112
Tel: Northern Ireland (028) 90233002

Marriage and Relationships Counselling Service (MRCS)
Tel: (01) 6785256
Fax: (01) 6785260
Website: www.mrcs.ie

PCI (Personal Counselling Institute) College
Tel: (01) 4642268

Family Life Service
Tel: (053) 9123086

Turning Point
Tel: (01) 2807888 or (01) 2800626

Church of Ireland Marriage Council
Tel: (01) 4978422

Kerry Counselling Centre
Tel: (066) 7122931

Kerry Adolescent Counselling Centre
Tel: (066) 7181333

Anne Dempsey
Tel: (01) 2874503

Muriel O'Toole PBVM, MIAHIP, ECP
Tel: (057) 8662101

Frances Heery MA MSc
Tel: (044) 9347395

Tara Counselling and Personal Development Centre
Tel: (028) 82250024

MEDIATION SERVICES
Family Mediation Service: under the auspices of the Family Support Agency
Tel: Dublin (01) 6344320
Tel: Limerick (061) 214310
Tel: Cork (021) 4252200
Tel: Galway (091) 509730

Julie McAuliffe
Tel: (01) 4903547 or (087) 7502428

Conflict Resolution & Mediation Consultants
Tel: (01) 2789897

Mediators Institute of Ireland
Tel: (01) 2017526

ALCOHOL ADDICTION SERVICES
Irish Association of Alcohol and Addiction
Counsellors
Tel: (01) 7979187

Alcohol Rehabilitation Centre
Tel: (01) 8641440

Alcoholics Anonymous
Tel: (01) 4538998

Al-Anon Alateen Family Groups
Tel: (01) 8732699

Stanhope Alcohol Service Centre
Tel: (01) 6773965

Cuan Mhuire, Athy
Tel: (059) 8631090

Rutland Centre Ltd
Tel: (01) 4946358

Addiction Counsellors are available at each local
Health Services Executive.

RECOMMENDED READING

Beer, Jennifer E. and Stief, Eileen (1987) *The Mediator's Handbook*, Gabriola Island, Canada: New Society Publishers.

Byrne, Tony, Maguire, Kathleen and Byrne, Brendan (2004) *Bullying in the Workplace, Home and School*, Dublin: Blackhall Publishing.

Crumbley, Joseph and Little, Robert L. (eds) (1997) *Relatives Raising Children: An Overview of Kinship Care*, Washington DC: CWLA Press.

Egan, Gerard (1990) *The Skilled Helper: a Systematic Approach to Effective Helping* (Fourth Edition), Pacific Grove, CA: Brooks/Cole Pub.

Elliott, Michele (1998) *Bullying* (Wise Guides) London: Hodder Children's Books.

Fisher, Roger and Ury, William (1991) *Getting to Yes: Negotiating Agreement Without Giving In*, London: Business Books.

Fitzgerald, David (1999) *Parents and the Bullying Problem: Understanding and Tackling Bullying: A Guide for Parents and Families,* Dublin: Blackhall Publishing.

Gladding, Samuel T. (2002) *Family Therapy: History, Theory, and Practice,* (Third Edition) Upper Saddle River, NJ: Merrill Prentice Hall.

Goddard, Trisha with Van Leeson, Terri, Gianfrancesco, Peter and Gianfrancesco, Billie (2003) *The Family Survival Guide*, London: Vermilion.

Goldenberg, Irene and Goldenberg, Herbert (2003) *Family Therapy: An Overview,* (Sixth Edition), Pacific Grove, CA: Brooks/Cole.

Higgs, Robert (2002) *What Have I Ever Done to You?* Cambridge: Pegasus.

Hollenbach, David (1979) *Claims in Conflict: Retrieving and Renewing the Catholic Human Rights Tradition*, New York: Paulist Press.

Kagan, Richard and Schlosberg, Shirley (1989) *Families in Perpetual Crisis*, London: WW Norton and Company.

Kelly, Kate (2003) *The Baffled Parents' Guide to Stopping Bad Behaviour*, London: Contemporary Books.

Kelly, Lorraine (2003) *Real Life Solutions*, London: Century.

Lawson, Sarah (1994) *Helping Children Cope with Bullying*, London: Sheldon Press.

Low, Abraham A. (1984) *Peace versus Power in the Family: Domestic Discord and Emotional Distress,* Winnetka, IL: Willett Publishing.

Markman, Howard, Stanley, Scott and Blumberg, Susan L. (2001) *Fighting for Your Marriage: Positive Steps for Preventing Divorce and Preserving a Lasting Love,* (Second Edition), San Francisco, CA: Jossey-Bass.

Markman, Howard, Stanley, Scott and Blumberg, Susan L. (2004) *Fighting for Your Marriage,* The PREP Approach videotapes, audiotapes and text-books on The Speaker–Listener Technique, Denver, CO: University of Denver.

Marr, Neil and Field, Tim (2001) *Bullycide: Death at Playtime,* Didcot, Oxfordshire: Success Unlimited.

Moore, Christopher W. (2003) *The Mediation Process: Practical Strategies for Resolving Conflict,* (Third Edition), San Francisco, CA: Jossey-Bass.

Morgan, Patricia (1999) *Farewell to the Family? Public Policy and Family Breakdown in Britain and the USA,* (Second Edition), London: The IEA.

Murray, Marie and Keane, Colm (1998) *The ABC of Bullying*, Dublin: Mercier Press.

O'Connor, Colm (2001) *Marital Counselling Research Project: Three Studies*, Dublin: Department of Social, Community and Family Affairs.

Ó Laighléis, Ré (1996) *Ecstasy and Other Stories*, Dublin: Poolbeg Press.

Pizzey, Erin, Shackleton, J. and Urwin, Peter (2000) *Women or Men – Who Are the Victims?* London: Civitas Institute for the Study of Civil Society.

Robinson, George and Maines, Barbara (2000) *Crying for Help – the No Blame Approach to Bullying*, Bristol: Lucky Duck Publishing.

Scanzoni, John (2000) *Designing Families: the Search for Self and Community in the Information Age,* Thousands Oaks, CA; London: Pine Forge Press.

Skolnick, Arlene S. and Skolnick, Jerome H. (2005) *Family in Transition: Rethinking Marriage, Sexuality, Child Rearing, and Family Organization,* (Thirteenth Edition), Boston, MA: Pearson, Allyn & Bacon.

Sullivan, Karen (2003) *How to Say 'No' and Mean it: Survival Skills for Parents,* London: Thorsons.